Love After...

I'M STILL STANDING

JACINTH HEADLAM

Love After...

Love After Copyright © 2018 by Jacinth Headlam
No part of this publication may be reproduced, distributed, or transmitted in any form or by any means, including photocopying, Recording, or other electronic or mechanical methods, without the prior written permission of the publisher, except in the case of brief quotations embodied in critical reviews and certain other noncommercial uses permitted by copyright law. All rights reserved.

I have tried to recreate events, locales and conversations from my memories of them. In order to maintain their anonymity in some instances, I have changed the names of individuals and places. I may have changed some identifying characteristics and details such as physical properties, occupations and places of residence. For permission requests, write to the publisher, addressed:
"Attention: Permissions Coordinator," at the address below.
Infinity Publications, LLC.
P.O.BOX 155
Woodstock, VA 22664
(540) 331-8713 or (202) 630-7323
www.infinitypublicationsllc.net

Book and Cover design by Infinity Publications, LLC.
ISBN-13: 978-1-7337349-1-2
ISBN-10: 1-7337349-1-0

Second Printing

10 9 8 7 6 5 4 3 2 1

This book was printed in the United States
All Scripture quotes are taken from the Holy Bible, King James Version, Cambridge, 1769; and The ESV® Bible
(The Holy Bible, English Standard Version®).
ESV® Text Edition: 2016. Copyright © 2001 by Crossway,
A publishing ministry of Good News Publishers.

JACINTH HEADLAM

TABLE OF CONTENTS

Dedication	4
Introduction	5
Chapter 1: How Did I Get Here?	6
Chapter 2: The Death of Divorce	10
Chapter 3: Dying to Self & Becoming Whole	19
Chapter 4: The Backstory of LOVE AFTER	34
Chapter 5: Power of Forgiveness	40
Chapter 6: Power Behind a Name Change	54
Chapter 7: What Is Your Purpose?	64
Chapter 8: Water Walking Experience	72
Chapter 9: Time to Maximize My Singleness	79
Chapter 10: Parenting After…	94
Chapter 11: Dating and Waiting	106
Chapter 12: It Was Necessary	118
Chapter 13: Birthing Your Purpose	125
Chapter 14: First Trimester of Purpose	128
Chapter 15: Second Trimester of Purpose	131
Chapter 16: Third Trimester of Purpose	137
Chapter 17: Taking Our Power Back	143
Chapter 18: The Power of Prayer	149
My Prayer	161
About the Author	163
Note From the Author	164
Credits	166

DEDICATION

I dedicate this book to conquerors who survived and resurrected from the death of their past. Past hurt, past addictions, past trials and tribulations, past betrayals, past shame, past guilt, and anything that tried to knock you down and take you out. I thank God you are still standing, healing and pursuing your journey of being whole and living out loud unapologetically. There is Love After…

God has the FINAL say!

JACINTH HEADLAM

INTRODUCTION

So many of us are struggling with past or present hurts, pains, traumas, betrayals, insecurities, addictions, and tribulations that blocks us from walking in our purpose and knowing our true identity. As you're reading this book, thank you so much for helping me birth my Love After vision. I allowed God to turn my pain into my purpose. I will assist you on how you too can use your pain to find your purpose.

Despite the circumstances that we've faced, there's Love After. There's Love After our addictions, shortcomings, emptiness, abuse, betrayals, abandonment, and brokenness.

Let's take this journey together, as we take back our power, overcome our deaths, and embrace the rebirth and resurrection of our purpose, love, vision, and identity. I want us all to live and love out loud unapologetically with our *Love After Glow*!

CHAPTER ONE

HOW DID I GET HERE?

I watched my faith and hope get stripped away from right before my eyes. At 29, I was living in my mama's attic with my two kids. We were sleeping on a full-sized bed and going through a divorce. I went from seeing my children daily to seeing them every other week. My mood at that time: *Depressed*; My feelings: *broken, lost* and *defeated*. All those emotions flooded me because I had lost myself, lost hope, lost faith, had no sense of direction. What is my next? Not to mention I didn't have a stable job because I wasn't the breadwinner in the marriage. How do I start over? I never thought that I would be the one going through a divorce. I questioned God, 'What happened to the new beginning that you promised me? God.... *Why me?*'

My three-year-old daughter Jenesis was supposed to be my new beginning: in motherhood, my marriage, my career, my spiritual walk, and my purpose. But that is not what was happening.

I just crawled into my bed and isolated myself

with the thoughts that there was not a single person in the world that would ever understand what I was going through. It didn't matter how many prayers I've received nor how many times I prayed; I felt as if God was not hearing me and had forgotten all about me. I felt so distant –as if I had fallen from grace. I just could not make sense of life and where I was, and for the life of me, I could not see the light at the end of the tunnel. Questioning myself became a norm for me. I constantly asked myself 'what did I do to deserve this and why was it so bad?'

After a 10-year relationship, of which nine were marital, I found myself going through the worst days ever. I found out through Facebook messenger that my husband had a baby on the way and this woman was nine months pregnant. Wow, just when I thought it couldn't get any worse! How in the world could I even begin to bounce back from this? We had just separated; the divorce proceedings had not yet begun.

As I said earlier, I went from seeing my kids every day to seeing them every other week. With them being involved in this, it made the situation worse. If it hadn't been for my kids, I probably would've packed up all my things and moved across the country or back to Jamaica.

Love After...

Every time I had to see him, whether it was dropping the kids off or picking them up, it was a constant reminder of the pain that I had to feel time and time again. Every day, I was constantly reliving or reminded of my painful past. Not only was I going to be without my kids for seven whole days, but they were spending those days at the other woman's house. He was living with her since we both moved out of our marital home and rented it because it wasn't selling.

Not only was this out of order, but messy and disrespectful!

1. Have you ever been in a place where you were caught off guard? Explain:

   _____
   _____
   _____

2. Do you find yourself questioning God or blaming God? Explain:

   _____
   _____
   _____

3. Do you feel as if this issue/situation will or will not work out for your good? Explain:

   _____
   _____
   _____

CHAPTER TWO

THE DEATH OF DIVORCE

What is death? No one can say for sure; however, I can attest that my divorce, was one of the worst deaths I've ever experienced in my life. *DIVORCE* rips away one's soul. It can be worse than an actual death because when someone dies you cry, grieve, bury the body, attend the funeral, say your goodbyes and with time, depending on the relationship, you learn to cope with that person's physical absence.

Think about it. When you marry a person, you marry their past, present, future, faults, trials, tribulations, shortcomings, failures, and even their successes. You become one...mentally, physically, spiritually, emotionally and sexually.

With the death of a divorce, I was recycling that death. Every time I saw my ex, flashbacks of all my hurts, pains, deceits, regrets and setbacks would rain down on me like a torrential rainstorm. I would then have to start all over, again and again, to piece my broken self back together again not knowing how we ever got to this place called *living hell*. Other experiences may have been extremely worse. I say '*may*' because having endured many traumatic experiences, I'm sure I developed a subconscious and temporary memory loss. My divorce was a constant resurrection of my death. It was mission critical that I began healing and restored my wholeness.

Dealing with the death of my divorce, I was battling finances, bankruptcy, custody, assets, bills, property, and you name it. I lost everything and hit rock bottom, having to start from scratch. I wouldn't wish this on my worst enemy. Depression snuck in like someone breaking and entering…in the daytime! I was sleepless too many nights to count. I was not eating well. I felt life was not worth living anymore. I was like the walking dead.

What played a massive part in my depression was not seeing my children every day. My norm was waking up to them every morning, making breakfast, lunch, and dinner, dropping them off at daycare and school, picking them up, tucking them in and kissing them goodnight. Suddenly, in the blink of an eye, it seemed like it was all wrongfully stolen from me. It felt like my chest was slashed open with a rusty, jagged edge knife and my heart was forcefully ripped out of my chest cavity while I was alive. Now I'm only allowed to see *my* children every other week. The week I was not able to see my children due to work and schedule conflicts were the worst days imaginable.

Then, it was unbearable to hear him say because I'm an artist with an unstable income, I might lose custody of my children. Divorce meant war. Not to mention before the ink was dry on the divorce papers, I found out that he had another woman around my children and they were spending the night at her house and eating her food. I didn't know if my children were fully protected or whether this lady was crazy.

The worst feeling was not being able to protect my children fully. When they were not in my care, I had to trust their dad's decisions, trust his judgment, and trust my children were in safe hands. Hands down, I can still say my kid's father is a great dad and very hands-on. Nevertheless, it didn't change my reaction because everything was new to me and I still felt that our split could've been handled in a more respectable way and with better timing for the sake of the children. If I was this affected by the divorce, I could only imagine how it affected our 9-year-old son and 5-year-old daughter. Everything was new for them as well, so we had to be very careful about what we expose them to, especially at such a young age.

When I went through my divorce, I learned so much about myself. I discovered I was never alone long enough to figure out who I was. So, if I was never allowed any *me* time, how could or would I learn to be complete? How would I learn to walk in my purpose without having self-doubts and feelings of inadequacy?

I got married at 21 years-old. I started dating my ex when I was only 19 years-old and boy oh boy, talk about the blind leading the blind. That was surely an understatement. We were the epitome of two babies learning how to crawl, walk, and wean ourselves from breast milk, if you will, on this journey called life. Learning about yourself while trying to understand someone else is a difficult mission.

It was just as daring as motorcycle stunts. What do you know at 19 years of age? Do you know what unconditional love is or how to receive and give it? I never really had a demonstration of what real love looks like, let alone feels like. Why? When I was growing up, I witnessed myriad divorces, arguments, violence, physical abuse, breakups, and makeups--way more

Love After...

than I can count. Looking back, I realize I rarely witnessed true love.

I thought that by staying in my marriage, despite how rocky it was at times and despite going through infidelities, I was breaking a plethora of generational curses by trying to save my family. I quickly learned that love could not be bought at any cost. I figured it was true and unconditional love because he bought me that huge, gorgeous house on two acres of land that I wanted so badly and he gave me a big, beautiful, upscale diamond ring.

When we had renewed our vows and were having our second child, I felt unequivocal that it was a confirmation of a fresh start. In my heart of hearts, I believed everything was going to be amazing, but that was short lived. I figured after having my daughter Jenesis, my new beginning; I was going to step out on faith and finish my master's degree and pursue my dreams as an actress. It was my time to finally cater to *me*. Who would have thought this leap of faith was going to lead to my divorce? In 2015, I started shooting as well as traveling for my first feature film in which I played the lead—the love interest who was an undercover cop. Now, you talk about the 'straw that broke the camel's back'?

JACINTH HEADLAM

My husband said he refused to be married to an actress. He reasoned that he did not fall in love with an actress nor marry an actress. He kept saying that when he married me, I had a stable job at the bank with a 401(k), benefits, and stability. He frowned upon me being an artist especially since I had to kiss the leading man on screen.

I felt it was very selfish of him. I supported his career in the military throughout its entirety. I dealt with the stress of his deployment to Afghanistan while being pregnant with our son, Jayden. I held down the family like a good wife is supposed to do. Now, it was time for him to pay it forward and support me while I pursued my dreams, but he was fiercely against it. We fought over my career path and began growing apart even more. I finally stood my ground and chose *me*. I could no longer live in someone else's shadow, sacrificing my happiness and heart's desires for theirs. I knew what my passion and dreams were, but I didn't really know what my life's purpose was.

I began my quest to figure that out. Many people think because you start loving yourself more, it means you start loving them less. My husband felt like I was going to find someone else in the entertainment industry who would understand me more than him. It turns out, he was starting to feel guilty about the hell he had put me through. That's not my guilt to carry, and I am not that kind of woman. So, I'm not accepting that. Let's face it, many of us don't like change nor embrace it. All I knew was how to be a wife and a mother, but *WHO WAS JACINTH?*

After being with someone for so many years, I had to learn who I was and how to embrace being single while finding my power. Being single ironically became a blessing in disguise. I was able to not only to spend time with the Lord, but make time for HIM. I learned to focus more on myself, my children, my purpose, and my journey. Most importantly, I got to focus more on being a better parent.

There's always room for evolution. I had to not only grow as a person but felt compelled to discover my true voice. I acquired a stronger foundation by building a closer relationship with God. I focused more on healing and seeking forgiveness from all my past deaths, hurts, and generational curses. In short, I focused on *being made whole.*

What sends us out of alignment is skipping the process of loving God and loving ourselves. Instead, we jump right into trying how to love someone else. We fool ourselves into believing that loving others and being with someone else will make us whole and complete. That's the wrong path, and I'm here to tell you that I am a living and breathing witness to attest to it.

You never want to seek someone or be in a relationship to feel complete. If you focus on building yourself up and staying focused; God will show you to your spouse, and your spouse will complement you and be in alignment with God's purpose for your life. Everything has its right time and place.

Your priority should be first to love God, then love yourself—only then, will you be able to love others unconditionally. You cannot love others, complement others, inspire others or be happy for someone else if you don't love yourself and are continually struggling with insecurities and low self-esteem. First, you need to know who you are.

In Matthew 22:37-40, the Lord says that the first and greatest commandment is to love the Lord with all your heart, mind and soul but just as equally and important, we are to love our neighbors as we love ourselves. Often many of us love our neighbors more than we love ourselves. And, sometimes, sadly, we love others more than we love God. Sometimes we submit

Love After...

to others' will and purpose for our lives and seek validation from others before seeking validation from God and submit to God's will for ourselves.

So, you can't figure out how to love someone in a relationship nor receive love or even truly give love if you don't know how to love yourself.

1. What are some things you need to die from, that may be preventing you from living your life to the fullest? Explain:

   _____

   _____

   _____

2. Are you willing to die to self? Explain:

   _____

   _____

   _____

3. What are the challenges that prevent you from living and growing past these self-deaths? Explain:

   _____

   _____

   _____

CHAPTER THREE

DYING TO SELF & BECOMING WHOLE

While you are going through your death experiences and transitioning, you will feel like something inside of you is dying. Hold on and don't be distracted by your current circumstances. No matter how good we all look, we all have issues that we are struggling with. I may look pretty and well put together now, but before I was a hot mess. I want to share how I got healed, how I got my breakthrough and released my shackles.

If God can do it for me, then He can do it for you. It's your time and your turn. Just step out on faith and Jump!

Try this exercise:

Reflect on all the deaths that you have experienced or are experiencing now. The feelings of hurt, pain, and trauma are excruciating. It's something that you wouldn't wish on your worst enemy. You can't eat or sleep. Here come those familiar feelings again: I'm broken, depressed, confused, hopeless, lifeless, and empty.

Love After...

Coupled with feeling mentally, physically, emotionally, and spiritually exhausted. Still not knowing what your next step should be.

On my journey of self-discovery, it was necessary for the old me to die in order to heal and be reborn. In order for you to find your true purpose, you must first *die to self*. Once I believed that God was truly in my life, I started to know who I am and what God intended for me. He helped me find my purpose. I want to share with you some of the exercises I did on my journey of soul searching.

Take a moment of silence and block out all the noise both externally and internally.

Breathe... Inhale.... Exhale.

Step 1: Make a list of everything you need to die from. Anything that's preventing you from growing and glowing. There's power in seeing the list on paper. So, you'll see clearly what's holding you back. Writing it down make everything real. The list will hold you accountable for healing.

Step 2: With these deaths (traumas, insecurities, struggles, trials) in mind, write a letter to the 8 year-old you. Feel free to use another age as a child that may be more personal and or powerful to you. Set time aside with no distractions and let your heart speak on your paper with no filters.

What do you want the younger you to know and discover while growing up? What you should know, avoid, or do to live a happy and healthy life (mind, body, and soul). Part of me always felt disappointed in myself. At one point, I couldn't forgive myself for some of the poor choices and decisions that I've made. I blamed myself for a long time, and I had to learn to forgive myself for not protecting the little girl inside of me while growing up. This letter to the younger me helped me to release a lot of baggage that was holding me down and captive, preventing me from living. This letter was the prerequisite for my self-forgiveness.

Step 3: Write a letter to the older you. Pick an age that's very significant to you. I would recommend twenty years older if you don't have an age in mind. Let yourself know what you're doing or about to do to overcome these deaths, trials, and tribulations so that you can live a healthy and peaceful life.

Love After...

If God had to take you home right now, you want to know without a doubt that you've lived a joyful and peaceful life.

In writing this letter, keep in mind what do you want people to remember most about you once you leave this Earth. Identify your dreams, your short-term and long-term goals. Identify your desired status for your spirituality, family, career, love, wealth, health, recreation, self-image, community contributions, etc.

This letter will keep you in alignment with your purpose. Identify all the fears that you plan to overcome in order to be purposeful and successful. It will hold you accountable to not give up or fail the older you. You can sign off on the letter, seal it, and put it in a safe place.

You can even email it to yourself. When necessary, you can read that letter as a reminder of your assignment, for self-motivation, and encouragement to keep pushing forward. The older you are banking on you to make him/her proud based on the choices and decisions you choose to make this day going forward.

These letters are therapeutic, motivating and powerful vehicles that will drive you to live a more inspirational and prosperous life. It allows you to take your power back and live out loud authentically and unapologetically.

Before I started my journey of healing and was going through my deaths, I literally ran out of options that would temporarily make me feel good. When I was at my wits' end, the Lord grabbed hold of me and cleaned me up.

I knew that for me to really be healed from these deaths, the one and only option that was possible was a relationship with the Lord. I prayed for God to teach me how to build an authentic and genuine relationship with Him. Most importantly, teach me the power of prayer and how to pray effectively. I didn't know the Bible inside out and I didn't know how to speak in my heavenly language/tongues, so I thought my prayers wouldn't be as effective.

I learned that God just simply wants a relationship with us and just wants us to communicate with Him daily in the ways we know possible. I first started by talking to God mostly in my car and in the shower. It was something about those two locations that made me feel more at peace and away from everyone and everything. I vowed to open my mind, knowledge, and understanding of how to comprehend the bible and how to effectively apply it to my life daily. I am not implying that I am perfect and a Bible genius because I am far from it. I am still and will always be a working progress.

God knows and sees your heart and will reward your faith, work, and progress. What's also important is that you get back up after you fall. You need to dust yourself off and try again. You only fail when you don't keep trying. Learn to trust God, yourself, and the process. When it comes to failure and progress, I've learned to have the mindset of a baby because babies don't care about failing. Babies/younger kids are fearless. They only worry about learning and growing. They fall, but they make the necessary adjustments and have fun getting up and trying again. The baby will learn by making constant adjustments. If we had that same mindset, how much further would we be in our lives?

My prayer, meditation, and devotionals started out once a week, and then it gradually increased as I matured in my faith and relationship with God. Then, I started to learn the power behind not only prayer but fasting. Fasting is denying your flesh and feeding your spirit. Fasting and prayer will help to put you in alignment to receive your breakthrough. Prayer and fasting will shift some things in your life miraculously beyond what you can imagine or ask for. If you want a supernatural breakthrough, try fasting and praying for just one day to start. Sacrifice and deprive yourself of all your fleshly desires and just pray and meditate on God's word and the things you want to see manifested in your life.

People tend to fear fasting, but miracles happen when we can shut the flesh down and submit. In my first round with fasting, I would do a couple of hours, then progress to half day, then to a full day. I've done fasting in which I didn't eat for certain length of time. I've also fasted from social media and television. Social media can be a huge distraction if not careful. It gives many of us the perception that if we're not booked or busy, we're not of importance or successful. Social Media is smoke and mirrors because some people use it to create a false perception of who they want people to believe they are and represent. It can prevent others from living in their truth with contentment by masking their true identity, feelings, and circumstances, with all these false or enhanced illusions.

Love After...

I am aware of what my weaknesses are, that can be very distracting to me. Fasting really helps me to clear my mind and detox from all my distractions.

You know what your personal distractions are, so fast accordingly. I seek God, so He can lead and guide me in my fasting. If you desire to know God's true purpose and intentions for your life, I dare you to step out on faith and seek Him in prayer and fasting. I've heard the saying, *if you want new results, you must be willing to do something different.*

As a direct result, you will finally begin to see things in your life unfold and manifest. It's a cliché, but you will see the light at the end of the tunnel. This is when you start entering your *Love After Death* phase.

You can finally breathe again. Breathe in hope, faith, love, positivity, forgiveness, humility and breathe out negativity, addictions, depression, suicidal thoughts, confusion, and insecurities. You will no longer cry tears of sorrow but tears of joy. Whatever doesn't kill you will make you stronger. Once you've had your Love After Death experience, you can be a blessing and pay it forward to someone else who will need to resurrect from their hurts and pains. Your trials and testimonies will be someone else's healing and deliverance.

God made you uniquely beautiful. Live out loud unapologetically. Be BOLD & BRAVE. Be original. Stop seeking validation. People will talk you out of what they can't make sense of and what they feel is too risky. Start discovering your voice. Once you realize that you are broken, you need to surrender to it to be made whole.

You may feel insecure, vulnerable, naked, delicate, worthless and not good enough. Allow God to use your flaws while He changes your mindset. This is where you have to be able to trust God on a deeper level like never before. At this moment I came the closest I've ever been with God.

I know what it feels like to be internally naked on all levels while allowing myself to be free. It is the most beautiful thing when you can see yourself evolve like a butterfly. Butterflies are so unique and fearless. To fly is freeing. I am now mounted up with wings like eagles.

To heal and to grow, first you must admit that you are broken. For an addict to be healed, they must first admit that they have the problem. In other words, one must own it. I had to own all my flaws and go to God ready to submit and lay all my burdens at His feet. Be intimate with yourself FIRST. The journey to wholeness and healing isn't an overnight process. It will take time to heal the brokenness and to develop the new and improved version of yourself.

I have several memories of the quick fix, pain replacements. Let me see; dating was one of them. Although I claimed to practice "waiting," I thought, 'hey there is no harm in dating.' I've learned that disobedience can cause you to lose everything. When God says wait, He means to wait. Other quick fixes included me working all the time because it kept me distracted with no time to dwell on my problems. Instead of dealing with my problems head-on, I was partying, getting high (smoking weed), and drinking. It made me feel as if I was free and on top of the world. However, that moment lasted until I returned home to the familiar four walls, and then, I was left alone to face my reality. That was a waste of money and time. I was usually left tired and broke with a hangover. Back to square one.

I found myself speaking to my friends about all my problems, instead of seeking God. Everyone's voice seemed to be giving advice, and yet, I refused to hear God's voice and His advice. In 2016, I was at the Fierce Divas pray women's conference and experienced a spiritual awakening. It was as if I was on a new dimension and crossing over into a new season in my life. This time, I feared to do it on my own. I feared God and didn't want to live this journey without Him even if I tried.

This feeling that came over me was one I have never felt before. I felt His presence on a different level. All I kept hearing him say was 'Welcome home daughter.' I felt comfort, love, and compassion and it was like a high that I didn't want to end. All I wanted to do was lay prostrate and worship Him. This new level of intimacy was better than sex, blunt, and my favorite foods. (Everybody who knows me, knows how much I love food. I am a big foodie—that's why my family calls me "Munchie.")

I've always loved God, but this time was different. I wanted to be deeply *in love* with Him. I wanted Him to be the apple of my eye with the cherry on top. I want Him to be my everything. I had a thirst and a hunger for Him that nothing and no one can fill or substitute. I officially started my journey to wholeness and healing. As we know, it is not a sprint --it's a marathon. But please know this journey and the wait-are worth it.

I started out by carving out daily, personal one-on- one time with God.

Love After...

With careful nourishment, relationships develop over time. I had to build intimacy with God. I know this may sound crazy, but there were times on my date with God that I put some music on and pretended to be dancing with him. I would close my eyes and waltz around my room with Him. You should try it; it will change your life. Even when I would go to church, it wasn't the same anymore. I wasn't just there because it was my norm. I was raised in a church and not going to church wasn't an option as a child. I was raised by my grandmother, Lucilda Jackson, in Jamaica. She was an evangelist, and we went to church religiously.

When I came to the US to live with my mother, she also went to church religiously. But this time it was a Seven Day Adventist church. Fast-forward to now, at 31 years-old: I can say honestly that I have finally developed a deep and intimate relationship with God.

For the first time, I have no issue with going to the altar and lay prostrate just to worship God for everything He had done, is doing, and about to do in my life. Whatever was weighing on me no longer mattered because once I submitted it to God and placed it in his hands, I now know I can trust Him through faith. I learned to live by the powerful four P's: **P**raise, **P**rayer, **P**ress, and **P**atience.

I learned that there is nothing too hard for God to handle. I now know what it's like to praise my way through and when that wasn't strong enough, I learned to pray my way through. When the devil tries even harder to defeat me, I continue to not only pray and praise, but I had to fight my way through by simply pressing forward. The one thing that I struggled with the most was patience. Believe it or not, patience was the hardest for me. We all want what we want when we want it, and we will not take no for an answer.

That's when I had to reprogram my mindset and continually tell myself, 'Ja it's not a sprint it's, a marathon.' In this season of my death and rebirth, I had to learn to completely and solely wait on God, as I mature spiritually in Him. The wait is not easy or simple, and I'll be lying if I said I've got it all figured out. I'm still working on it. However, I have learned the power of waiting on God and His divine timing. When it is God's will, and you're in alignment, it's like everything falls into place effortlessly.

I started to learn His will versus my will. I feared being out of alignment with His will for my life.
If anything threatened my peace of mind, I ran in the complete opposite direction. If anyone knows me, they can say *'Ja don't play with her peace of mind.'* If

anything causes me to second-guess, waiver or more importantly give me a headache, I'm exiting stage left. That's when I learned to stand still and be in control of my energy and atmosphere.

In dying to myself, I had to learn to love myself unconditionally. We always talk about loving others unconditionally, but it is very rare that we flip that around to loving ourselves completely without barriers. When you can love yourself unconditionally, you will become more secure and will learn to have standards. You will no longer settle for anyone who cannot love you unconditionally, flaws and all. Learn to love yourself past your deaths. It's time to resurrect and walk in your new identity. To take off your old layers and walk in newness.

Walk with a *Love After Glow*!

Things I had to die from:
- My divorce
- Unforgiveness & Resentfulness
- Feelings of inadequacy
- Depression
- Suicidal Thoughts
- Procrastination
- Fear of the Unknown
- My post-pregnancy stretchmarks & my scars
- Masking to cover-up my pain & vulnerability
- Drinking Alcohol to numb or escape my pain
- Carrying baggage and deadweight

God plan is to prosper you and not to harm you. He is here to give you hope, a future and peace. Not insecurity and doubt. You must first be whole and healed from your brokenness by dying to self. Walk in your newness with your *Love After Glow*!

CHAPTER FOUR

THE BACKSTORY OF LOVE AFTER

There was a time in my life when I felt lost, broken, confused, with no hope or sense of direction. The greatest loss that I've ever experienced was losing self. I gave up on my dreams of being an actress and became a wife and a mother. Not that I am complaining about it, but I began to feel stagnant and like I was on a merry go round with my life and out of alignment. One day I laid prostrate right on my living room floor and cried out to God. I became fully ready to surrender and seek His direction. I found myself saying *'YES to Your will; YES, I'll obey, I'm tired of existing. I want to live! I want to walk in my purpose in you!'*

Then it hit me. **WAIT!** What is my purpose? Many people have their dreams, passions, and aspirations, but are unsure of how that ties in with their purpose. I've always dreamed of being an entrepreneur, mentor, and an actress/model. One day, as I was on a soul-searching awakening journey to discover my purpose, it came to me: Love After Death! It was so clear.

It's mind-blowing because, on this particular day, I had my awakening while I was taking a shower. God can speak to us at any time and in any place.

My response was, 'God how is this my purpose?' He said, "I want you to turn your pains into your purpose. Allow me to heal those broken wounds and make you whole. I know you've been hurt, I know you've been betrayed, I know life has knocked you down, and you don't feel you can trust or love again. Daughter, there is Love after these deaths. I want you to bury all of these deaths and be renewed and resurrected to what I've called you to be.

Some things need to be buried such as your insecurities, infidelities, betrayals, depression, suicidal thoughts, confusion, doubts, deceit, double-mindedness, molestation, abandonment, your old perception/views of love and life. Allow Me to use your pain, trials, and tribulations as a testimony that works out for your good. In this, you will come face to face with your purpose, and I will get the glory..."

I was a little apprehensive because I know that the *Love After Death* vision would require openness, transparency, and vulnerability about my personal life. My thoughts wandered, and questions were raised.

Love After...

How can I air my dirty laundry?

I thought, God, I don't understand, but I'll trust You. Of course, it wasn't that simple. Out of fear, I allowed the vision to lay dormant for a year. Once again, I found myself in the same spot: stuck, stagnant, and going in circles. I began to fast, pray, and cry out to God for direction and clarity. He clearly stated, "Daughter you are committing spiritual suicide. I told you what your purpose is and in that is where your breakthrough lies. Remember, to whom much is given, from Him, much is required. Faith without works is dead." Like many of us, I wanted God to bless me with my heart desires but without doing the work or at no cost. I was fearful of allowing people to see my nakedness, vulnerability, hurt, and pain. I never liked anyone to see me sweat.

Then, one day it was like the floodgates of heaven opened up, and God took away all my fears. I finally embraced my journey to healing and was ready for the real work to begin. I started praying, fasting, worshipping, learning how to meditate and control my energy. I began reading His Holy Word and became transformed by the renewing of my mind. As I grew in my relationship with God, I became bolder, fearless, and started to live out loud unapologetically. I was in a new space in my life. I was ready to walk in my purpose. I was finally prepared to give birth to my *Love After* vision that was given to me by God.

I began journaling, created The Love After Facebook page and created my vision board. God started sending me the tools, resources, and support systems that He knew I needed for this vision to manifest. I finally grasped what it meant to be in alignment. What I thought was my greatest loss became my greatest blessing.

My identity is through God. The enemy doesn't want us knowing who we are, whose we are, or how powerful we are. We are above and not beneath, the lender and not the borrower. We are who God called us to be. It is time to stop seeking validation from people who don't even know who they are. Stop taking on perceptions of who the world thinks you are or supposed to be. Who you are is according to the word of God which is your "Truth."

It is impossible to know who you are if you don't know whose you belong to. God wants to use all of us. He wants to use every part of us, but that can only happen if you know your true identity.

Love After...

I had to go through a season of my life where I had to learn about myself all over again. I had to learn what my true identity was after I lost myself. But first, I had to heal.

So, if you are lost, let God reveal to you who He created you to be. Have you ever been in a position where you find yourself asking:

God, where are You? Why is this happening to me?
I did what you told me to do, so where did I go wrong?

1. Describe a moment in your life when you lost your identity? Explain:

   _____
   _____
   _____

2. Describe a time in your life when you felt like giving up and like no one cared or understood you? Explain:

   _____
   _____
   _____

3. Have you ever felt like you're stuck in that gray area of your life?

_____
_____
_____

4. Explain your feelings and emotions during those times.

_____
_____
_____

Love After...

CHAPTER FIVE

POWER OF FORGIVENESS

For a while, I allowed unforgiveness to keep me from fully healing and becoming whole. Forgiving is one of the hardest things to do, but it's the prerequisite for God to start moving in your life. I've learned over the years that forgiveness is a gift to yourself. When I forgive you, it's not about you; it's about me becoming free. I'm freeing myself to go to my next level. Don't allow unforgiveness to rob you of your peace and hold you back from your destiny! Do you trust God to let go and forget the past?

God will create new things in you. He can only fill empty spaces. So, learn to make room for Him to fill you up. God wants you to spring forth something new in your life. God wants you to birth new visions, new dreams, new blessings, but you first must allow Him to penetrate you with His love and His grace. If He's doing a new thing, there has to be a new you?

His love can create a new attitude, a new spirit, a new mindset, new heart, new love, new faith, new trust. Ask God daily to create in you a clean heart.

Create a new atmosphere. You can't go into your new season with old habits. God wants to lead you into a season of abundance. Stop putting a cap or a ceiling on God's blessings. There can't be fear in that space. TRUST HIM to renew you. Allow God into your life to move and shift things around.

God wants to bless you, but your old habits are often blocking your blessings. Ask God to show you what doesn't need to stay with you in your new season. Listen and watch what He shows and tells you. He may challenge you about your heart, your mind, your relationships, your giving, your habits, your dishonesty, and your lack of transparency.

If you're open to change and accept the challenge to grow new in Him, the shift will take place. He will reveal everything to you if you allow Him to. Reveal to Him the old relationships and old habits that are not welcome in the new season. Ask God to purge and purify your heart. He'll create in us a clean heart and a renewed mind.

I had to make a conscious effort to forgive those who did me wrong or hurt me. I won't forget what these people did because it is the learning experience that molded me into the woman that I am today. Although I didn't get the apology that I needed or deserved, I still had to forgive to get the peace of mind that I needed to be whole and to heal. For example, I forgave my ex-husband and prayed for prosperity over his life in all areas. His happiness and health do affect our kids. Despite what we've been through, he's still family, and I want nothing but the best for both of us.

Another forgiveness milestone that was very hard for me was when I finally forgave my older cousin who molested me when I was eight years old. This was a death that laid dormant for years. I blamed myself for years because I felt like I should've spoken up and I should've said something to my grandmother who was my guardian in Jamaica at the time, while my parents were both in the United States. I wondered, did I fight hard enough? Did he feel it was okay to take advantage of me? Did he think I liked it because I just laid there, numb, confused, and lifeless?

All these questions were based on the lies I kept telling myself. So, I just owned up to it and never dealt with it until I started writing this book. Although I feel uncomfortable writing this, I must stand in my truth to help someone else who might have gone through or is going through what I've gone through. In healing from this, I wrote a forgiveness letter to him, just as a release and relief for me. I never gave it to him, but it gave me the closure I was praying for.

Then, I told my mom about the situation. Her calm reaction wasn't what I was expecting. I guess she didn't want me to see how much it affected her. I later heard from my aunt that my mom called her crying about the news I shared with her. My aunt also told me that my mom confronted him and told him he needs to apologize to me. I never got an apology call, letter, or a visit from him. Whether I receive an apology or not, I still forgave him, and I am at peace and can finally move forward.

I also had to learn to forgive myself. I was no longer a victim but a Victor, claiming victory over ALL my circumstances. I was no longer living in regret. I was bolder, more confident, more optimistic and more of a risk taker. I was tired of living in the regret of not leaving my marriage when I had the chance, due to the worst humiliating infidelity anyone can experience. Not only was I hurt and betrayed by my ex-husband, but I was also hurt and betrayed by someone I loved dearly like a sister.

The betrayal forced me to question myself and

Love After...

my worth. Why did I stay? Did I not love myself enough to think I deserved better? Did I not trust God enough to restore me?

I had all the power in my hands to leave, but we all know it's easier said than done. My decision to stay in my marriage was because of the covenant I had with not only my ex-husband but also with God. I knew there's nothing too hard for God to fix. I wanted God to show up and show out in my marriage. When children are involved, it's much harder to walk away. I wanted my kids to have the complete family that I never had growing up. But at what cost?

I also feared failure and didn't want to be another divorce statistic. Growing up, we never witnessed examples of a stable household or what a great and healthy marriage looked like. Not to mention we were both so young and didn't know what love is. I knew love from what I was taught, told, read, witnessed and saw on television. That's all I had as a reference. Growing up, I had only witnessed toxic marriages and relationships.

When I relocated to the States and started living with my mother, and my stepdad at the time, all I witnessed was my mom getting abused physically, emotionally, verbally and mentally. I still remember this one incident clear as day. My stepdad locked them both in her bedroom. All I heard was my mom crying out in pain as he beats on her. All I could do was call 911, while panicking and crying. The moment he opened the door, I took the first thing I could grab at the moment-- which was a frying pan-- and hit him in the head with anger and rage, as he ran out the door.

By the time the cop got there, my stepdad was already long gone. All we could do was file another police report and get a restraining order. I'm sure the cops at our local police department had our address memorized. It didn't matter, because days later he was back in the house, fearless as if nothing happened. Then the same cycle would repeat itself. I was only a child, and no matter how much I hated what was happening, all I could do was keep quiet and respect their marriage. I had to stay in my lane as a child. Everything was great Monday to Thursday. Finally, I had the family I prayed for. But, by Friday when he got paid, he'd get high, drunk, and spiral out of control. The worst and scariest incident that I witnessed was him holding a knife to my mom's neck threatening to kill her.

Love After...

Although I love my mom, for a while, I was angry at her for not choosing herself, her happiness, safety, and her health over his. I know it's easier said than done. Love is very blind. When you're not whole, and you're broken, you will attract what you are. I finally get it, now that I'm older and more mature. She wasn't whole and complete. She never witnessed a healthy, and stable marriage growing up. She did the best she could. She's now divorced, healed and has found love and life after her deaths within herself. She finally learned to choose herself first and have a deeper relationship with God.

I am no longer living in regret of my divorce and my poor choices and actions. I'm no longer living in the brokenness of being molested. My life drastically changed when I stopped living in the past. I had a new attitude called wholeness. I was no longer incomplete or relying on other things to make me complete. The only thing that could fill that empty void was my Lord God Almighty.

In forgiving myself, I also had to stop living in should've, could've, would've. I've learned to move on and fully accept and embrace the new me. It is so easy to fall back into old habits and old patterns. Stop living in who you were and live for who you are and who you'll become. Forget past pain and guilt. Grow and learn from it then let it go! My past prevented me from moving forward and became an excuse for my inability to grow.

People will think that you've changed or you're acting funny, you're acting different, or you're not yourself anymore. You didn't change, you've improved, and your priorities changed. Not everyone you start with will finish with you. Which was one of the hardest things I had to learn. For me, loyalty is everything. I've always given people the benefit of the doubt. Once I love you, I rock with you because I love hard. I can now love and pray for you from a distance. The new me had to L.I.G.-- learn to (Let It Go!) and K.I.M. (Keep It Moving!)

I want everything that God has in store for me, and if that requires me standing naked before Him, flaws and all, or it requires me to die to myself, then I'm ready. My prayers are for God to use me how He sees fit. Cleanse me and give me a renewed mind and a renewed heart. Change the lens through which I view life. I love what God said in 1 Samuel 16:7(NCV), *"That he doesn't see things the way we see them. People judge by outward appearance, but the Lord looks at our heart."* This scripture has taught me how to love and view others based on God's lens.

I made a vow to myself to never allow anyone to force me to take my crown off. I will always keep my crown on and walk with grace and dignity. I want to live out loud unapologetically. I no longer will bask in self-pity or wear the victim sash. I will no longer get lost in my anger and bitterness because of my past. My past is not who I am. My prayer every day is for God to change my identity and help me to walk more in the likeness of His image and whatever His calling is on my life.

It's time to break all generational curses. Have you paid close attention to the way you versus the prior generation handle offenses? Does your mom or dad avoid difficult situations? Do they prefer not to confront uncomfortable issues at the roots? Forgiveness comes to us naturally. Think about it, if we yell at our kids or spank our children for their wrongdoings or as a disciplinary action, they'll turn around and hug us and allow us to embrace them like nothing ever happened. That's because as kids, their mind is pure and for them forgiveness is natural. You will never find a baby or a child holding onto resentment because you spanked their butt five minutes ago.

Unforgiveness is something that shapes and molds us as we get older. This is a perfect example of nature versus nurture. When growing up, I always witnessed my family yelling and storming out of the house every time something went wrong, or things didn't go their way. As I got older, I noticed a similar pattern of how I handled my offenses-- by avoiding, isolating and running from the issue.

That's an example of nurture. Unforgiveness is a defense mechanism and learned behavior. Unforgiveness has taught us that this is the best way to protect ourselves, to defend ourselves, to guard our hearts, and to let you know #IAin'tTheOne.

Unforgiveness doesn't hurt the offender or your enemy; it hurts *you*. You're blocking your blessings and committing spiritual suicide.

Looking back, I began to regret the times I ever argued with my ex in front of our kids because I now admit I was teaching my children the wrong way to solve problems. I wish I would've let many things go and take the high road. We should have waited until we were both calm and level-headed to have a more mature conversation. Reacting out of feelings and emotions is not an effective way to communicate.

Love After...

I could've chosen to pray about the situation, instead of taking off my crown and acting immature to get my point across. I was fighting a pointless battle. To learn how to communicate effectively, we started going through marriage counseling, which I would recommend to any couple struggling in their relationship. One tool that we've learned, that I still use today is the time-out method. We use *'time outs'* to guide children, but taking time out to control yourself and your emotions is a very effective strategy.

Taking time out will prevent you from saying or doing hurtful things you can't take back. Taking time to cool down, gather your thoughts and emotions, and return to have a healthy discussion out of love, is a beautiful thing. Sometimes you may not have all the right words, but you can ask your partner to join you in prayer instead. If you have nothing good to say, it's best to say nothing at all.

You must renew your mindset, change your perspective and reshape the way you view your offenses and your offender / your enemy. It brings us back to the cliché "when life gives you lemons make lemonade." When you change the way you look at things, you'll see the enemy coming from a mile away. You can start stretching and prepping for positive change. You'll be doing a lot of bobbing and dodging by not letting anything stick on you, rob you of your joy and your happiness, take away your peace or bring you down.

No matter what the enemy throws at you, just let it go. The Lord said in His word, "all things work together for your good." He also stated that "no weapon formed against you shall prosper." I have learned to trust God and stand on His promises.

Like me, you have two choices when someone offends you. I can either allow it to take me out of my character, to take me from 0 to 100 very quick, and to go all the way off the rails. The other option is, I can choose to go about it the peaceful way and let go, allow God to take control, and handle it on my behalf. Most of the time, the same people who offended you are the same people that will come right back around and cry for your help, for your forgiveness, and need you to rescue them.

When the Lord says that, *"He will prepare a table before you in the presence of your enemies,"* he was not lying. I have witnessed this scripture come to fruition time and time, repeatedly in my life. That's why all things will work together for your good.

Love After...

That's the good the bad and the ugly. It will all make sense in due time.

When you release and let it go, you can make more room for God to bless you. How can God take you to your next level and a new dimension if you're still weighted down with baggage and walking around with shackles on your mind? You can't fly with dead weight. You can't run with chains on your legs. What God has in store for you is way bigger and better than what is behind you. Stop looking back and concentrate on moving forward and let it all go. Free your mind, free your energy and free up your life.

Many people say they forgive but still hold on to bitterness and resentment. This is where dying to self plays a considerable part. God wants you to live a life of abundance. He wants to see you blossom and live your life unapologetically. Do you want to fly high and embrace your destiny or do you want to drown in your history and generational curses and patterns?

If you do not find the grace to let it go, or find it in your heart to forgive, you will limit your blessings and block your breakthroughs. You will feel lifeless and stuck. You will always be struggling, lacking peace, lacking joy and only experience temporary happiness.

JACINTH HEADLAM

Try this exercise:

1. Write a Forgiveness letter to everyone you'd like to forgive, even yourself. Be very descriptive of the situation and how it made you feel. Write about the hurt, guilt, pain, deceits, disappointments, betrayals, anger and feeling ashamed. Write with the intention of letting it go and moving forward. Practicing forgiveness as the key to living a fruitful life filled with joy, peace, wholeness, and happiness.

2. Once you've written the letter(s), you can choose to rip it up, shred it or burn it. Choose the best method that symbolizes a release and moving forward. It's done, and it's time to celebrate your rebirth.

CHAPTER SIX

POWER BEHIND A NAME CHANGE

When my divorce was final, I had to learn how to use my lemons to make lemonade. One of those lemons was my name change. *"I'm going back to my maiden name, Headlam,"* and unbeknownst to me, it would soon be a life awakening period at that very moment of my existence.

At one point, I felt as if I was being pulled back from going forward by strong rip tides. The harder I swam towards the shore of newness, the more I was being pulled back into an empty shoreline. That's when I snapped out of it. I realized there was power in a name and my power was linked to my name change. I was reminded at that moment how God had changed the names of some of His most influential prophets in the Bible. That's when I started to embrace my name change like a Boss.

Think about it. There are some very important and influential people in the Bible that God used and eventually changed their names in order to take them into their next seasons and reach a new level in Him.

The name change represented their new identity and a new creation. For example, Abraham's name was initially Abram. God changed Abram's name, meaning "*high father*," to "*Abraham,*" meaning "*father of many*" (Genesis 17:5). God changed Abraham's wife's name from "*Sarai,*" meaning "*my princess,*" to "*Sarah,*" meaning "*mother of nations.*" In the New Testament, Jesus changed Simon's name, meaning "*God has heard,*" to "*Peter,*" meaning "*Rock*" when He first called him as a disciple (John 1:42).
They BOSSED UP & LEVELED UP!

My name change was a *new identity* and my new beginning. I was finally able to *exhale*. It is a way to reveal the divine plan and to assure that God's plan would be fulfilled in me. They stood on God's promises. Changing from my married name back to my maiden name not only gave me an opportunity to make changes, but to break generational curses from my childhood that has taken until now to come full circle because I didn't have the courage or understanding to do so before. God took me back to my Genesis; my new beginning in Him. He gave me a fresh start and a second chance to make things right by shifting some things in my life. I died and transformed from the person I was, to become the person that God has called me to be. Instead of waking up dead, I was reborn and woke up alive. My soul was rejuvenated, and most importantly, I was thankful to still be alive.

All the things that the enemy knows that you like-- he will make extra attractive to you. It'll cause you to waiver, be double-minded and have the spirit of confusion. If you don't understand or know the way, just ask God to show you. Show you the way and the path that He has for you. Having a relationship with God is essential. Once you have a relationship, you will then have the wisdom about what to do and how to handle life's journey and struggles. You'll also have the wisdom on what to say, how to say it and most important, when to say it.

Your destiny is bigger than you. You'll always have a choice to live or die. We all will get to a point in our life in which we'll have to decide when to make a stand. When is enough enough? Stand like Esther who is another Boss and Queen I admire.

Esther was a woman of virtue in my eyes. Esther's former name was Hadassah. Esther was a true and faithful servant. She was willing to die to self to save her people. Esther knew that her *yes* was bigger than her. Her willingness and obedience saved an entire nation. Esther was chosen for such a time and timing is everything. Esther was selected as Queen to fulfill God's purpose. She was chosen for a specific reason. It wasn't about her; it was about Him. God has a plan for each of us, and we must wait for His direction and His leading. We must also be vigilant when called. If we do not answer the call, God may call someone else.

Your obedience is not about you. Your purpose is not about you. You don't have to be perfect, super holy, the best prayer warrior, know the Bible inside out or be super gifted, to be used by God. This was what I once thought. Yet, God has used some of the most flawed and imperfect individuals to do mighty things. You have some people who would think, act, or say they're holy, but they're no earthly good, and they walk around being masked. You know the saying all too well, 'a wolf in sheep's clothing.'

All it takes is to simply create an intimate relationship with God. God wants a relationship with you. He wants to be the love of your life. He wants to be your *everything*. He wants to be your best friend.

I could've been easily dubbed the fastest mara-

Love After...

thon runner.

I kept running away from my calling and my purpose because I, too, had the mindset that I had to be super holy, with perfect posture and articulate speech, and not have any flaws to be used by God and not feel ashamed.

However, a part of our purpose is by using our flaws and our testimonies to help others. In having a relationship with God, you have to trust Him and ride it out on pure faith. Many people will say, *yes, I have a relationship with God,* yet you do not even trust Him. Instead, you'd rather put your trust and faith in man more than Him. You allow others' voices, including your own, to be louder than His voice and direction.

I always wonder how having no relationship with our creator interferes with the relationships we have with our children, our spouses, our parents, and our loved ones? If you think about it, sometimes we are too busy for God and too busy to have time for our kids. In life, it's all about relationships and how you balance and prioritize these relationships.

I've always struggled with balancing various acts. Sometimes when you get overwhelmed, and you put a lot of time and energy into your job or business, it does interfere with the time you put into your relationships. One thing I wish I could've done differently in the past was to have spent more time nurturing my relationship with my spouse. Of course, many factors played a part into why I chose not to after I checked out, but that doesn't make it right. When you don't care anymore, the marriage is over.

Regardless of what your spouse has done wrong in the union, if you choose to stay, you need to give everything your best, leaving no stones unturned. If you're choosing to stay-- then serve, sacrifice, be selfless and give it your all regardless. Once again, our obedience is not about us but to God, our commitment, and the covenant that we've made by choice.

You can't continue to hold on to bitterness, resentment, and hurt. Put everything in God's hands and let Him handle it. Just focus on doing the work, and He'll make provisions. He Knows exactly what you need, and He knows what's best for you. He created you, molded you, and know every single number of strands on each of our heads. He wakes us up each morning, and He's the reason why we are breathing and have blood flowing through our veins.

How can we put more faith in others who can't

Love After...

even give us life?

The minute you begin to take your eyes off God and stop allowing Him to lead you is the minute you begin to lose focus. You start to feel lost, overwhelmed and inadequate. Therefore, you lose your sound mind and begin making rash judgments and poor decisions. We all must get to a point in our lives where we are intentional about our *Father's* business, and we're intentional about choosing life and not death.

Choose to walk with your head held high and not hung down low. Choose to be the victor and say *no* you will no longer be the victim. Choose to live every day like it's your last because tomorrow is not promised. Live your best life now and to the fullest while hoping to see tomorrow. Every morning that I wake up, I am so ever grateful for another day to get it right and another chance to live vibrantly. I'm granted God's mercy and grace, despite my flaws and shortcomings. Through building a strong relationship with God, I have learned to trust Him and not lean on my own understanding. He said in all your ways acknowledge Him, and He will direct your path.

The enemy's job is to divide, conquer, kill, steal, and to destroy you. He wants division in your home, on your job, in your relationships, and especially in your marriage. When a home doesn't have both parents, it creates an automatic imbalance. Often, these broken individuals have trouble bouncing back, and as a direct result, these individuals walk around filled with anger, resentment, and unforgiveness in their hearts as I stated in my chapter on forgiveness.

You have come too far to allow the enemy to destroy you. Allow God to strengthen you and to sharpen your spiritual eyes by giving you a stronger spirit of discernment. To not be blindsided, it is mission critical to change your thinking. Come up with a strategic plan to look ahead and bob and weave to avoid obstacles. You will then learn to think and move wiser and smarter.

As a result, you will not be infected by the enemy's poison nor buffeted by your storms. You will be able to get up, dust yourself off and pick yourself up after you fall. As you step out on faith and stand for something so that you will fall for nothing, God will strengthen you, equip you and reward your faith.

Love After...

Paul said in Philippians 4:13 *that I can do ALL things through Christ who strengthens me.* There's no limit on His strength. You will be strengthened through your storms and sorrows. He will strengthen you over and over making you Teflon-coated, so you can rise up and keep standing.

Note your Thoughts:

1. How far are you willing to go to sacrifice for others? Explain:

_____
_____
_____

2. How far are you willing to go to fulfill your purpose?

_____
_____
_____

3. Are you willing to say yes to God, despite your circumstances?

_____
_____
_____

4. Since our trials are our testimonies, who do you think can learn from your mistakes and testimonies?

(ex: Kids, abused men or women, raped victims, divorced, incarcerated, newlyweds, gang-related, etc.)

_____

_____

_____

Love After...

CHAPTER SEVEN

WHAT IS YOUR PURPOSE?

Many people do not know or understand what their purpose in life is. How do you know whether you are walking in your purpose or not? Well, if this question brought uncertainty, it could be that you are not walking in your purpose or unaware of what your purpose is.

Are you lacking peace of mind, joy, and excitement about living? If you are waking up every day not feeling thankful and dreading the rest of the day or week--then you're not excited about living.

Most likely, you are not walking in your purpose. If you continuously overwork yourself merely to avoid facing life, you are avoiding your purpose. I know many people who purposely overwork because it keeps them busy and prevents their mind from thinking about the burdens of their lives.

Working too hard lets you avoid facing your issues head-on. When you are super busy and going in circles you deliberately have no time to find your true purpose. There's no sense of growth or movement in the right direction. You feel lost, broken into millions of pieces with no sense of direction. We all know people—and often ourselves—who suffer from ADS—*Always Doing Something*—to avoid sitting quietly to seek the truth.

Finding your purpose allows you to live a meaningful life. Finding your purpose requires a journey of self-discovery. Try seeking Intimacy (In-to-me-see) with God. Try to search deep within yourself. Open your mind, knowledge, and understanding so you can expand your thinking. By becoming open-minded, you can eliminate worry and confusion--both tricks of the enemy. There are multiple activities and pursuits you can follow that align with your purpose. Keep in mind that your purpose is not someone else's purpose. What God has planned for you is just for *you*.

Some people's purpose is revealed over time as they begin exploring their gifts, talents, passions and heart's desires. Sometimes, we are distracted by materialistic things and other's success. Always remember that you are uniquely and wonderfully made. Embrace all of you, flaws and all. Feeling fulfilled spiritually, not materially, will help you find the ultimate happiness that you've been continuously seeking.

Love After...

A good number of people are still seeking their purpose. You are not alone. However, ask yourself if you are looking for your purpose in a spouse, in money, in your career, in your success, in your relationships, in material gains? Try looking for your purpose from the One who possesses your purpose. Most of us have that microwave oven mentality and want everything in the blink of an eye. When you plant a seed, you don't water it thinking the next morning it will miraculously grow into a fully-bloomed plant overnight.

Seeds take time to grow. They require water, sunshine and nourishment to flourish. Most importantly, growth takes time. But, many of us are unwilling to be patient because we are so distracted, lost or have no sense of direction. A purposeful life is not a sprint; it's a marathon.

Think about the most horrible life experiences that you've been through that you never thought you could get past or healed from. Reflect back on the times you didn't feel like life was worth living. You probably found yourself getting angry at God, at your offenders, over your offenses, and mad at yourself for allowing certain things to happen to you.

Well, I am here to tell you, that's where your

purpose lies. Your mission is to be a part of the solution to a problem. You are an answer and a missing puzzle piece in this puzzle called life. Right now, ask yourself: what area(s) in your life have you grown the most in which you feel you can be used as an instrument to be a blessing and help someone else who struggles with the same issues you've struggled with?

If God can bless me, keep me by extending His Grace and Mercies upon me, surely, He can and will do the same for you. You must ask yourself, am I ready to be a SERVANT? If you are ready to serve, then you are prepared to walk in your purpose. Purpose = Serving, Sacrifice, and Selflessness.

I am interceding on behalf of everyone reading this book. I believe that your blessings and breakthroughs are right behind your YES, your submission to His will, and your selflessness. Are you ready to finally start living and not just exist? Are you prepared to live life to the fullest and be all you were predestined to be? Even if you haven't been through many trials and tribulations, ask God, how can you use your passion, gifts, talents, and aspirations to be a blessing to others and to give back to your community or the world. Devote time to finding your passion. Sit quietly and think about some things you are passionate about. Ask yourself right now, if money wasn't an issue, would you still do it regardless if you were not being paid? Ask yourself: are the things or activities I do every day necessary? Are they the key to truly living a purposeful life? The most critical piece of the puzzle is trusting God. Trust God for direction, for having faith, hope, and working hard. Trusting God through the good, the bad, and the ugly is the key to walking in your purpose. I had to trust Him and put Him first before I began walking in my purpose and following my dreams and visions.

If God gave you the vision, then the provision is on *the* way. Sometimes people want to inject their own or other's opinions into God's plans. You must refuse the temptations of being distracted by other people's thoughts, their advice, opinions, attitudes, agendas, motives, and most importantly, their judgments. God is the only one who appointed me. Therefore, I must obey Him and align in His will. I can't afford to detour from my destiny. We must continuously remind ourselves that God is able. Every time I'm going through my struggles, there's one song that gets me through catastrophic times. The song, *He's Able* by

Deitrick Haddon had me laid out on the floor bawling my eyes out and ready to surrender everything to God.

He's a promise keeper. I can say, most of the visions and goals that I have, some have already manifested, and I am beginning to see Him answer the others as my story unfolds. Just trust God. He's able and willing to do exceedingly and abundantly above all that we can fathom to ask, think, or even imagine. Take a moment and thank God for His services in your life and for His infinite Grace, Mercy, and Favor for serving you and keeping you even when you think you may not have deserved it.

Try these Vision exercises:

A huge stepping stone that motivated me to walk in my purpose was to start writing out my visions and goals. Create a Vision Board reflecting where you want your life to be in a month, a year or even ten years. According to *Habakkuk 2:2*, God wants you to write down the vision; write it clearly. Set some goals and deadlines. Put your notes somewhere visible like on a mirror. So, every time you wake up, it will remind you and hold you accountable. Write your vision on a piece of paper and put it under your pillow or inside your Bible. Another option is to put it under your favorite cup so every time you drink from that cup, you are reminded to drink your dreams daily. These methods are mind-blowing and will help you to focus and prioritize. We spend so much time living to exist versus walking in our purpose.

Many people have probably said to you that you'd never become or amount to anything and that you'll never get far in life. Someone may have told you that you're too old or too young to accomplish certain things and that you've missed your mark. Some will say you're not smart enough or anything enough. Don't listen to them. It's time to start creating your own history--not just read about history makers. You can create your own history by walking in your purpose. God specializes in taking all our brokenness and our messes and molding them all together for *His* glory. Now it's time to tell your story and make history.

Time to Reflect:

1. What are some of the most horrible life experiences that you've been through that you never thought you could get past or heal from? Explain:

   _____
   _____
   _____

2. Are you prepared to live life to the fullest and be all you were predestined to be? Explain:

   _____
   _____
   _____

3. What are you passionate about? Explain:

   _____
   _____
   _____

4. What are some trials you can use as your testimony for your purpose? Explain:

   _____
   _____
   _____

Love After...

CHAPTER EIGHT

WATER WALKING EXPERIENCE

Just like Peter I had my water walking experience. One of the hardest decisions I ever had to make was taking that first step. I remember every day going to work at the bank feeling lifeless. I felt empty as if I was just existing.

My legs felt like I was walking through cement from the time I left my car in the parking lot to the time I walked into the building. I felt like I was being held hostage for eight hours a day. Every day, Monday through Friday, for those long eight hours I wasn't living; I wasn't breathing; I couldn't even be present. I was lifeless, and it was time for a change.

Every time I thought about quitting and starting a new chapter in my life and career, I was overwhelmed with uncertainty. I was scared to admit it, but I knew in order to move forward, I had to recognize my fears and overcome my shortcomings. I didn't know what to do about maintaining stability, since I was a mom and a wife at the time. If I quit my job, how would I pay all my bills and my tuition?

However, I felt something strongly calling to me. It was God's voice saying, "It is time to get out of the boat Jacinth and trust me."

It was on a Sunday, my late great pastor Diana Wright at Liberty Worship Center, preached a sermon that was so profound. The title of her sermon was right on time for me. That's right you guessed it: *Water Walkers*. That message was and still is the best sermon I've ever heard, and to this day it still holds so much power and value in my life. It has guided me through all areas of my life; through the good, the bad and the ugly.

I remember like it was yesterday when she was saying, *"God is calling you to get off the wall, step out on faith and be a water walker. Anything that's holding you back on that wall you need to leave it in that boat. Step out and be a water walker!"*

It was that message that gave me my first step toward learning how to start living a purposeful life. After numerous years of yearning to be at peace, I was no longer obligated to walk around on pins and needles inhaling and holding my breath with every step. Then it happened. I was able to exhale unapologetically after

Love After...

waiting so many years to finally be at peace with letting go. My entire being was immediately filled with tranquility, peace, and love with no more worries. I had to let go, let God, and take a leap of faith to step out of the boat and walk on my water of fear, inadequacy, insecurity, seeking validation, people pleasing, and so forth. That following week was my last week working at the bank. It was at that very moment I began pursuing my dreams of being an actress.

You must ask yourself, *"what do you want people to remember about you?"* I want people to know me as a *water walker*--someone who inspires and motivates them to follow their dreams. Someone to help others find and walk in their purpose.

Following God's purpose for your life while using your gifts to bless others is what life is all about. My 'ah ha' moment was realizing that my purpose had nothing to do with me. My purpose was for a higher cause. Our purpose is being an answer to a problem, to people's prayers, and being a blessing to others. At one point I felt like yes, I'm finally doing what I love. I'm living my dreams out loud as well as following my dreams. However, I still didn't feel fulfilled. I still felt a void that needed to be filled. Whose purpose was I following, mine or God's? This is what I pray for, and it is finally starting to manifest, but something still didn't feel right. As I began to build a closer relationship with God, I had to learn how to submit to His will. I was pursuing my heart desires without any respect to His will and trusting His timing. I found myself trying to jump ahead of God. Who was I fooling? I was continuously falling on my face or steadily bumping my head.

As I grew in my faith and as my relationship became deeper and stronger with God, I began hearing His voice louder and clearer. He now shows me things in the spirit. I finally figured it out. I had to submit to His will and His way for my life or else I was going to keep on spinning my wheels.

Having faith is not about believing in God to get what you want exactly when you want it. Faith is believing that God will give you what you need in His divine timing according to His will. *"Faith is the substance of things hoped for, the evidence of things not seen"* (Hebrews 11:1). So, if you can't see it or feel it, will you still trust God? Your blessings may be delayed, but it's never denied. Ask yourself this, if God granted you all your blessings and heart desires right now will you be able to handle what comes with that.

Remember to much is given, much is required. At every level you grow to, there's a different devil. Will you be able to handle the pressure that comes with all these blessings or are you still immature and underdeveloped?

In the right time and right season, God will complete what He told you He would do. For you to know God's will for your life, you must be obedient and read His word, which is the truth in which we are to live. His will is revealed in His word. It took me a while to get into my word and allow it to meditate on my heart because I didn't want to live with boundaries according to His words. I was so used to doing things I was already comfortable doing. We must get out of our comfort zone to get in touch with our spiritual zone -- which can be uncomfortable. However, in the end, it is well worth the challenges related to a dramatic transition.

Praying was easier for me than following the Bible. It was a struggle especially because I lacked spiritual maturity, due to the fact I was so lost. I would justify my wrongdoings by saying, *"God knows my heart."* I had to learn the task of setting boundaries. Boundaries were necessary because it allows you to stop being distracted.

It gives you a standard that sets the precedence on becoming more focused on your *purpose.*

Sometimes I found it challenging being a water walker and not be distracted. Our 20/20 vision gets blurry preventing us from seeing past our circumstances. Life can get you to the point where everything becomes not only a blur but sometimes a blank. You don't know what's next for your life. You can't see the light at the end of the tunnel, and you don't know how to make your dreams a reality. How to get back your 20/20 vision is by seeing life through God's lens. Trust His direction through the Holy Spirit. He left us a comforter.

It's impossible to see clearly and have a 20/20 vision if you're living in darkness. Are you living a life that is positive and that will bear good fruit? If you're not living a life that you're proud of, then it's time for a change and transition so that you can be able to see in the light and no longer live in darkness. If you don't deal with the darkness in your life, it will manifest and grow like an out of control parasite. It will interfere with your interpersonal relationships and your connections and begin to infect others. You must be careful how you entertain strangers and how you treat people because you never know who is tied to your destiny.

We must pay close attention to what we focus on daily because what you focus on is what you magnify in your life. So, if God is not a huge focus in your life, He will not shine or be a reflection of your life. What you're regularly feeding your soul and your spirit is what your life will reflect.

I want God's purpose for me to be a reflection and help me daily to be a woman of wisdom, inspiration, and excellence for all to see. I want to inspire others to walk with power and authority.

I want you to aspire to be a Water Walker.

CHAPTER NINE

TIME TO MAXIMIZE MY SINGLENESS

Being single is just as important and powerful as being married. There's power in both lifestyles. Being single is not a negative or a punishment for not being married. I was able to become more confident and find my purpose while single. I had to accept that being single does not mean that I feel lonely or lonesome. We all think the ultimate goal is to one day marry your life partner.

However, it's wrong to worship marriage and or feel so desperate to be married that you lose yourself and fail to fulfill your wholeness by first finding your true self as a single person. Throw away the timeline for marriage. You'll only feel frustrated. Date yourself first and learn to love yourself by focusing on your positive qualities. Deepen your connection with God and build a healthy relationship with Him first.

Being single opened my eyes and gave me the opportunity to see God at His best. If I was still married, I would've just thought my breakthrough was coming from God blessing the covenant. However, when I felt

Love After...

God bless little ole' me despite my shortcomings, I was able to see God at His best and keeping His promises. Also, I began to solely rely on God. For the first time in my life, I wasn't relying on a husband, my mother, my grandmother, friends, validation, opinions or T.D. Jakes, my spiritual father. I was relying on God. When I was in my Valley the only one that I could've relied on, called on, and depended on was God. It was during my darkest hours when I experienced God's grace, mercy and His favor on my life.

Timing and preparation are everything!
So many of us are so consumed with wanting to get married. Especially women. We were raised with the belief that one day our Prince Charming will ride in on his white horse, in his shining armor or our Boaz will find us in the fields.

1. Take a moment to think about these questions:
   Are you prepared for your spouse if you both crossed paths today? Explain How:

   _____
   _____
   _____

2. Are you prepared to share your entire life with someone else and to selflessly take on their burdens as well? Explain How:

_____
_____
_____

3. Is your half complete and content before marriage? Explain:

_____
_____
_____

4. Would you even marry yourself? Explain Why:

_____
_____
_____

5. Did you conquer your power in your singleness? Explain:

_____
_____
_____

Love After...

I asked these questions because we often carry old emotional baggage we haven't dealt with or old wounds that are bandaged and not fully healed. So, we aren't emotionally prepared to be in a healthy relationship.

If your heart and mind are festering with unforgiveness, traumas, and abandonment issues from mommy, daddy, or loved ones, you need to heal from these issues before starting a new relationship. A relationship will unmask these issues and bring them to the surface. Then, instead of your partner enjoying the new union, he or she ends up carrying your baggage. This can cause you both to grow weary and feel exhausted. Now, a fresh, new relationship is no longer enjoyable, and you've grown apart.

Many of us don't know what love is or how to love. Therefore, how can you find it possible to love someone else when you can't even love yourself. That's why being whole while single and waiting on God to bless you with your spouse is so important. It will eliminate or minimize a lot of the issues we face in our relationships. It won't remove them all together, but it will eliminate the unnecessary ones. That's why I chose to maximize my singleness by not dating or pursuing a relationship. After exiting a ten-year relationship, I was still under construction. I couldn't entertain the idea of getting married so soon. I wouldn't have been able to see my partner's value because I wasn't fully healed. In maximizing my singleness, I took the necessary time to die to self and become whole again. *It's not fair for someone else to serve the time for someone else's crime.* Through God's grace and mercy, I am now more prepared for marriage again, but most importantly I'm at complete peace with waiting on God's divine timing as I continue to grow in my wholeness.

In my singleness, I am also preparing for how to be more intimate and affectionate by practicing with my relationship with God. In the past, I've struggled with showing or being affectionate. Growing up, it was rare that I witnessed my Caribbean family show affection by hugging, kissing, or saying "I love you." Their way of showing love was making sure we had shelter, delicious homecooked meals, and our basic daily needs were covered. So, I thought if my husband was fed, the house was clean, kids were taken care of, and his sexual needs were met, I was doing a good job. I only knew how to be romantically affectionate when I was horny or wanted something. Looking back, I now

Love After...

realize this was a pattern I had to break in order to have a successful relationship. I didn't want my kids to follow these generational patterns of lacking affection. I want to be more loving and affectionate at all times. I want to show affection even when it doesn't lead to me being sexually satisfied.

When the time is right for me to get married, I want my husband to feel respected, loved, cherished, honored, and to know that he's my top priority. Romantic or simple gestures to show your love, appreciation, and affection has a massive, positive effect on your relationship.

From what I've witnessed, most people think being single is tough, but I believe you should enjoy your singleness. Being single is a gift and a beautiful thing when managed appropriately and effectively. Being single gives you the time to become whole without feeling incomplete. You can use this time to focus on being the best version of yourself, instead of looking for an upgraded version of your ex.

Being single, I've learned to be in alignment and enjoy my freedom. Not having to answer to anyone, you have more free time to open a business, to go back to school and pursue your dreams. I found it tough to balance all these things while being in a committed relationship and being a parent to young children.

I'm not saying it's impossible to do it all. I've done it in the past and have been on both sides. Being single gave me more freedom to explore my gifts and perfect my craft.

The more people in your household, the more you're pulled in all these different directions with additional responsibilities. Kids pull you in one direction, and your spouse pulls you in another. Marriage is hard work. I felt like it was like having a full-time job and then working a graveyard shift. I salute married couples who can make it work and find balance. To make it through two, five, and ten years, I applaud you. Past 20 years-- blow some horns. I salute and respect you all because I know what it takes, and it is hard work. It speaks volume and tells me that you're selfless and have sacrificed a lot. A successful long-term relationship often requires putting your personal happiness on the back burner temporarily.

I've learned, you don't become a wife or a husband when you say "*I do*" or when he put a ring on it. You become a wife or a husband before you meet your life partner by first becoming a spouse in your spirit with God. That's when the preparation starts. If you can't submit to God in obedience, then how can you be obedient in your marriage? Proverbs 18:22, it states, "*He who finds a wife finds a good thing and obtains favor from the Lord.*" So, ladies, we have to be a wife with our crown already on before our king finds us. There's a reason why God stated that, he who finds a *wife* and not he who finds a girlfriend or fiancé'. You are his good thing, and in marrying you, there are certain favors that he'll obtain for the covenant and his family. Ladies, we are powerful!

    A relationship is like a seed. You can't expect it to grow and blossom if you don't provide rich soil and water it. It's very dangerous if a person searches for someone to fill a void. Instead, seek someone to compliment you. It's best when you take this journey with someone who's also whole. It's important not to compete with each other. Often, couples get together and find themselves competing in their marriage or relationship. This leads to jealousy, envy, and animosity which is very tough to overcome.

    I know many women who complain about their partner because they've settled for a man with a boy-like mentality who aren't kings and who don't know who they are or how to lead. Same for men who settle for women who aren't queens and not prepared to be a wife. Too often, we get married based on hormones, feelings, religion and lust. To find real success, you must be led by God because he'll let you know when you're ready to marry.

After the wedding is when you really begin to exercise that true selfless, submissive love. When you think about it, we start falling in love with God after we get in a relationship with Him. That's when we got to know Him and become more in tune with Him. After marriage and living together is when you really find the true meaning of loving that person. You can't be in love with someone you don't know. You never know a person inside out until you're both living under the same roof. That's when you're put to the ultimate test. That person begins to see you on all levels, flaws and all. Marriage exposes every part of you. Marriage will expose our nakedness while forcing us to be vulnerable.

Married at a young age, all I knew was how to be a wife and a mom. I started pursuing modeling at 17. Then when I started college, I began to slow down and then I stopped pursuing my dreams. While in college I

Love After...

got married at 21 and had my first child at 22. I was a student, a wife, a mom, and active in the church's artistic ministry. Although I've graduated, the advice I would have given the younger me would be to enjoy your youth and her college life to the fullest. I wish I had gone away to college and explore what it would be like to live in a college dorm. These are major milestones that prepare you for adulthood that I can't get back. Although I have no regrets, this is the advice I would give another young lady.

I felt lost, being pulled in all these different directions at such a young age. After my divorce, I had to put in the necessary work to find myself and my identity. I had to put a lot of work into healing and becoming whole. After finally forgiving my ex-husband, I no longer pointed fingers or placed blame. I realized that we were both kids in grownup bodies. We were both incomplete and lost. The blind leading the blind. We've made a lot of mistakes that should have been made while dating and transitioning into adulthood.

We were two kids who weren't whole and still learning how to walk with the limp life threw at us. We stumbled a lot while learning to walk on our journey. However, we are now mature enough to know we were unhappy together, but vow to be the best co-parent we can be for our kids.

If you are single by choice or by divorce, God wants you to grow in your singleness. Many people feel they can't fully embrace and walk in their purpose without a spouse. You can definitely be just as powerful and walk in your purpose without marriage. Look at Jesus and Paul. They did it. Why can't we?

Marriage is a beautiful thing. However, before you start dating or seeking to be married, first you must date yourself. Have many date nights with yourself. Pamper yourself. Love and splurge on yourself, while living and budgeting within your means. Making intelligent decisions is essential. Be careful not to idolize or make decisions based on money and materialistic things. Financial discipline and learning the true meaning of stewardship is also necessary. How do you manage and prioritize your blessings?

When you are busy with improving yourself, you'll notice you don't have time to waste. You will not have room to entertain nonsense. When you're complete and whole, you will find yourself becoming choosier with higher standards and expectations and refusing to settle.

Love After...

Your energy will be very sensitive to things that are not prosperous. You will be high on life and walking in your purpose. You will set the necessary boundaries and have standards to have a successful marriage or a successful single relationship with yourself. With God's love come boundaries and limits.

Like any parent, you're going to set rules, boundaries, and limits for your kids out of love. You don't want your kids to go down the wrong path or hurt themselves. Having boundaries was necessary because it allowed me to stop being distracted, it gave me standards, and I became more focus. Many of us got hurt in our relationships because we did not set standards, boundaries, or limitations. So, if you find yourself interested in someone and neither of you have boundaries, it will be a messy situation.

To maximize your singleness is also to maximize your time. Being single, I now have more time to spend with God. Our relationship is the strongest it has ever been. I am loving and appreciating Jacinth like never before. In this season, I've learned that I needed to be more selfish with my time and energy.

The times that I've wasted and had nothing to show for it are being put back into rebuilding myself from scratch. I was able to put more time into growing my business. I was able to put more time into dating myself without having to take anyone else into consideration prematurely. I don't have to rearrange my life for someone else until the time is right.

I was able to date my kids and spend more time with them. Take them to some of their favorite places and have mommy date-night. With help from my mother, my siblings, their father, my grandma, and my dad, I can travel frequently and work as hard and long as I want to without feeling guilty and hearing negative remarks.

In my new life, I learned that it's also important to exercise your mind, body, and soul. Exercising reduces stress, improves longevity, and gives you boost of confidence. Exercise your mind by reading more books to expand your horizons. Learn to meditate and find your peace and power within. Be more conscious of your health and fitness by exercising and eating properly.

I'm here to say that it is not selfish to put you first and to make yourself a priority. Don't allow others to make you feel guilty for prioritizing your well-being and your mental, physical, emotional and spiritual

Love After...

health. Allow the peace of God to guard your heart and mind. Don't allow your mind to be intoxicated by anyone or anything. Ask God to assist you in guarding and protecting your heart and mind.

Try this exercise:

1. Select one day weekly for Self-Dates.

What are some ideas you have in mind for your date night to yourself?

_____

_____

_____

(I've chosen Mondays to be my self-date day. On this day I tend to go to the hair & nail salon, the spa, the movies, seafood restaurant, etc.)

2. Purchase yourself a promise ring and wear it daily as a constant reminder to value and love yourself unconditionally. It'll keep you accountable to never settle for safe. It's a promise to wait on God to send your life partner who will someday replace that ring and complement your life and be in alignment with your purpose. It's a promise never to lose faith and hope, and to never be overwhelmed by fear or worries. This special ring symbolizes peace, joy, power, healing, wholeness, and will give you a *Love After* glow.

JACINTH HEADLAM

For this exercise, I bought myself a beautiful rose gold Diamonique® ring that was very inexpensive (less than $100). Since I model for Diamonique® on QVC, I can tell you their diamond-like rings are beautiful, high quality, sparkly, affordable, weighty and it also comes with a warranty. This is a great place to start for your first promise ring. I am in love with my Diamonique® promise ring.

CHAPTER TEN

PARENTING AFTER...

Parenting after divorce can be complicated because there is no way to avoid each other. When you first split up, you hope to never see your ex another day in your life--but that's impossible when kids are involved. Although you are no longer married or in a relationship, you're still stuck in each other's lives long-term.

The transition from being a married mom with a complete family to being divorced and a single mom was very challenging. My main concern during my transition was how would this divorce affect my kids. Children vary in their responses to divorce. Some children like the fact that their parents finally got a divorce because of how unhappy and miserable they all were.

Once you've separated, everyone can have a fresh start. The former couple is usually happier, and the kid(s) are more at peace. Many people underestimate how much kid(s) can pick up on your lack of peace and happiness.

Some parents try not to argue in front of their kids and think by keeping tensions on the down low, the kids won't notice. That's their way of trying to protect the kids. Kids are way smarter than we think. Just like adults, kids pick up on energy and spirits, too. They know the difference between true happiness and the negative energy of unhappiness.

Some kids can become depressed, unhappy, and struggle with getting used to their new normal. Some kids may have to move away from their Norm and start all over. My kids had to re-enroll in a new elementary school, relocate to a new neighborhood, make new friends, and get accustomed to a new way of living. Their standard of living also decreased. They went from a big, family-sized house with a huge backyard to living in an apartment. Now they have to tiptoe, so they don't disturb the neighbors downstairs. At first, it was hard to balance because, in a complete family household, there's help and shared responsibilities. Fast-forward to now, I carry all the responsibilities in my home by myself.

There's no such thing as shifting the load. I'm responsible for it all: making sure all the bills are paid, dinner is cooked, homework is done, laundry is done, the house is cleaned… after working all day.

Love After...

If something breaks in the home or car need fixing, I am now fully responsible. Thank God, I am somewhat handy.

Finding a rhythm and communicating effectively as co-parents can be very challenging at first. It is not healthy to have your kids be the middleman or the messenger between you and your ex. As adults, we have to be able to put our feelings and emotions aside and have a healthy communicating relationship.

Even if you don't feel like communicating, please do it for the sake of the kids. You must communicate openly, directly, and respectfully with the other parent. Being on the same page when it comes to the kid's schedule is very crucial. If you're in a place where it's hard for you both to communicate, there's an amazing scheduling tool that you can use called Family Wizard (www.OurFamilyWizard.com).

You're still communicating but not directly. It'll outline the schedule for the kids, game times, practices, scouts, etc. Other family members like grandparents, attorneys, babysitters, can all have access to this online tool as well. Also, you can just stick to emailing each other, so nothing important is lost in translation. It's an easy and effective way to track communications.

Creating boundaries has a huge impact on your co-parenting relationship. As I stated before, it's not healthy for your child or children to feel torn between their parents because you ask them to be in the middle or be the messenger. It's not fair to question your child about everything that happens while he/she is staying at dad's or mom's house. This only creates additional stress and tension.

I'm speaking from experience because my kid's dad and I had to learn to trust each other's parenting skills and know that our kids are our number one priority. I just wanted to make sure my kids were safe and comfortable when not under my supervision, but I had to trust and respect his time with our kids. I now have stronger and more effective communication skills with my kids, where they feel very open and comfortable telling me about their experiences, good or bad, without tension or pointing fingers or making their dad a factor. We solely focused on their experience, their thoughts, and what life is like through their lens. Co-parenting is not about us-- it's about our kids and making the best decisions for them together as a team based on love and respect.

Although my divorce was my new beginning, the

process can be mentally, emotionally, and financially draining at first. At that moment, you may also see a side of your spouse you've never seen before or knew existed and vice versa. To some, divorce means war and is far from cordial. When kids are involved, vulnerability and fear of losing your child or children can cause the gloves to come off.

Divorce also has a significant impact on kids emotionally and mentally. Although my kids' behavior didn't change, as their mom, I can still pick up the burden they carried in their spirit. Especially my son who's older and couldn't understand or make sense of everything. They've tried to make sense of why we couldn't live in the big house we just bought. There's no perfect way for me to explain everything to them. I proceeded to tell them, *"Mommy and Daddy are no longer together, and for us to be happy, we have to live separately and start over. Mommy and daddy are going to put on our capes and work hard to make sure that you both have the best life possible."* It still wasn't a good enough explanation. All they knew was that their world was turned upside down.

My son always asked, why his dad and I can't get back together, why he had to start a new school, and stated how much he hated switching homes every week. Then, to make matters worse, my son started getting bullied by twin brothers on the school bus at his new school. One day, the bullying led to my son's head being shoved into the school bus window, causing him to get a cut on his forehead.

As a mom, seeing him in pain, both physical and emotional, was disheartening and the worst feeling I've ever felt. I felt hopeless, angry, defeated, and started to blame myself at first. Thank God I was in my right mind because I could have acted out of anger and gone to jail. To make a long story short, it led to the police getting involved and meetings with the school principal. I still feel that the school system is unfair and doesn't have a proper procedure to deal with bullying. The kid who bullied my son was moved to a different seat with no disciplinary action or suspension. Thank God, I was able to get him enrolled in the same school as my daughter, so he was given a fresh start. As a parent, you want their world to be perfect, but that's not their reality. I only have control over their world part of the time. I work hard to make it perfect to the best of my ability during the weeks that I have them. My worst times ever are when I have to go an entire week without seeing my kids.

Love After...

It's tough to not be able to pop in whenever I want to just to say *'hi'* and to hug them because I still have to respect our mutual boundaries. I don't mention all of this to scare you because I am proof that there's Love After divorce and separation. I just want to give you some insights about my experiences and the adjustments I had to make by sharing the pros and cons.

On the positive side, once I got used to the rhythm of caring for my kids every other week, I had to find something to keep me occupied, so I am not drowning in my tears while they're away. I now have more time to binge watch all my favorite TV shows and movies. I now have more time to focus on my career without feeling guilty. I can work as long and hard as I'd like without having to rush home to cook dinner or help with homework. Not seeing my kids daily forced me to appreciate the times we are together even more. I think the distance and the time away from them created even a tighter bond. They have learned not to take the parent they are living with for granted because they hated not seeing both of us daily. I have become more intentional in having date nights with my kids and planning more bonding activities. I have grown to appreciate my family and friends even more because without having them as my support system, I don't know how I would manage.

Dating as a parent can be challenging as well. We all want to someday meet the love of our life, but the unknown can be scary. That's why it is crucial for me to date with my antennas on high alert. My children are my first priority, and I would never date someone or put myself in a situation that's unhealthy or harmful for them.

It's not easy to introduce your child to a new man or woman that you're dating exclusively. I'm sure it's tough for any child to get to know someone entirely new and different from their parents. Pacing and timing are very important in dating. Make sure you're healed and utterly ready to date before you take a leap. Some parents move on too quickly and have not yet fully healed or closed one door before opening another. This is where a lot of parents make the wrong decisions in dating. They move too fast without getting to know the other person long enough before introducing their kid(s). This can lead to molestation, rape, rebelliousness or verbal, physical or emotional abuse. Love is blind, and if you're not careful, you can easily sacrifice your kids for the sake of wanting to be in a relationship, by any means necessary.

Love After...

Having a tight bond and a strong relationship with your kid(s) is necessary. I am very connected with my kids not just emotionally, but spiritually. So, if something is off or wrong with them, I know instantly, and we have open dialogue and prayer about everything. I work hard to avoid making careless decisions that will interfere with my healing and my relationship with my kids. To that end, I took a break from dating to focus on my journey of wholeness with no noise or distractions. Any blessing worth having requires hard work, dedication, and selflessness.

Post-divorce, I found more time to focus on me, my kids, and the areas in which I struggle. My village played a considerable role in my healing. I am grateful for all the encouragements, help, advice, and prayers from my families, friends, and church family that got me through this time.

I'm excited that my son and I are receiving professional counseling. (If your insurance doesn't cover counseling, there are agencies like the United Way that provides counseling on a sliding scale). By talking to my son about his thoughts and feelings, he told me he wanted to speak to a male therapist about everything he's going through with the divorce and at his school. Having an honest dialogue with your child is very necessary. Adults are not the only ones who go through the divorce. Kids are affected just as much as we are, if not more. The journey of healing and wholeness is necessary for both the parents and their kids.

I joined a divorce connect group at my church which has been very therapeutic because I get to hear about other journeys. Their stories remind me that I am not alone, and it could always be worse.

I've learned to trust God, count it all joy, be grateful, and to stop living in fear with doubts. There is nothing too hard for God. Just trust Him and lean on Him. If we're going to be changed, we must renew our mindset. If we're going to change and be transformed, it must happen in the spirit of our mind.

We have to be more intuitive with our kids. Practicing happiness, patience, leadership, friendship, and communication with our kid(s) is so important.

We have to date our kids and love the hell out of them. I know sometimes they drive us crazy, but nothing can replace the love we have for our kid(s) as parents. That's the blessing of parenthood.

Love After...

Reflection:

1. How did your kid(s) or step kid(s) handle the divorce? Explain:

_____
_____
_____

2. Did you carry the blame of the divorce interrupting the kid's life? Explain:

_____
_____
_____

3. How did you release the guilt of the divorce and the effect it had on your kid(s)? Explain:

_____
_____
_____

4. How was dating as a single parent?

_____
_____
_____

5. How did your kid(s) react to your partner and adjust to the new relationship?

_____
_____
_____

There is Life, Joy, Happiness, and Love After.

Love After...

CHAPTER ELEVEN

DATING AND WAITING

I had to learn to reshape and transform my perception of love, how to be loved, how to receive love, and how to recognize real love. I've grown to learn that my lens and perception of love was so tainted from my past experiences. What I've learned to be love was false and not the correct way of how I needed to be loved. Learning how to love and mastering self-love comes from within.

In loving yourself, you must have standards, and set boundaries because you will attract what you pray for. You will attract what you need. You will attract whatever it is that's on the inside that reflects outwardly. I've been praying to God to help me to receive love, but most importantly, to receive love as I've never received it before. Most importantly, help me to give love unconditionally as I've never given it before.

It's very challenging for a broken or hurt individual to maintain a healthy relationship. Hurt people hurt people. You're going to bare the fruits of what lies inwardly. You'll always find yourself looking for someone who can carry the weight of your pain, if you are not careful. That is why I had to take the necessary time that I needed to heal, become whole, and be complete.

I've tried dating through online dating sites to get my feet wet since it has been ten years since I've dated. The challenge is, I am more of a traditional woman in a microwave society. I've come across some great gentlemen who were great potential mates. I've learned some men don't take the proper time to court a woman like they should if they are truly interested in her. I've been fortunate to date a couple of great guys. We shared great chemistry and connection. We were equally yoked, they complemented my life, have solid morals and a relationship with God, but the timing was off.

I began to seek God for clarity and direction because I couldn't make sense of the uneasiness in my spirit despite their strong potential. That's when God revealed to me that He needed all of my time with no distractions. He instructed me to stand still while He prepares me for marriage. By dating, I realized that I needed to take some more time to date myself. There

Love After...

was still some hurt that was still lying dormant that I didn't know still existed.

So, I have taken the necessary steps to not only date myself but to build more intimacy with God. By developing a great and intimate relationship with God, I know he will release me when it's time to fly, to open my heart and let someone into my world. I will not only know how to receive his love, but I will be able to give love wholeheartedly and unconditionally. I will be able to put the necessary time into studying my new man --learning his love languages, triggers, and what makes him glow with joy. Until then, I vow to stand still with peace as I trust God for my next season, my new love, my king. I will be whole, complete, and ready for him to complement my world as I will his.

After a ten-year relationship, it's the season to be selfish with my time and love on me more. I knew deep down that I wasn't ready for a new relationship because in this season I am in love with dating me more. It would be selfish of me to wrongfully lead someone on and block their blessings if I know I am not ready for a relationship. In this season of singleness and healing, God has shown me so much about myself that I never knew existed. I know when my king finds me, I'll be the best investment he'll ever make. I'll be not only his good thing, but his best thing.

I never could make sense of why as women we try to save everyone. We are natural nurturers and we birth life into this world. Without our existence, there's no life. Women we are powerful. However, why is it that as women we always believe in others more than they believe in themselves? We fall in love with their potential and the good we see in them that they sometimes don't see in themselves. When a woman thinks she's in love, she tends to think more with her heart and not her mind. I can boldly declare that love is blind. When a woman is in love, they tend to give too much too soon. Ladies, if we're not careful, we'll find ourselves seeking a project instead of a partner. Most women won't wait on the right partner because they rather rush to fix a few faults and make him a partner. Some women settle and feel like it's an honor to at least have a man in their life rather than no man at all.

My advice is to perfect what God has placed inside of you. You'll always have potential mates, but finding the right one to cultivate you, complement you, and whose purpose is in alignment with yours will come with God's timing. It will happen when you least

Love After...

expect it and most of all it'll be peaceful and effortless. You won't have the *but* statements, and you won't have to seek validations and confirmations from others as to whether he or she is "the one." If you have to question the relationship and feel the spirit of confusion, then that person is not reflecting where you're heading in your life. You don't have to say, *"I love him/her, but...I don't know."* That statement alone should alert you that he or she is not the one.

When you discover the right one, you'll stand boldly; ready to profess your love to the world for the person without second-guessing or wavering. Until then, don't settle. Take as much time as needed to work on you, date you, learn you, explore the world, travel more, and live life to the fullest. Trust God's timing and trust that He knows what's best for you. Don't get discouraged because there's definitely LOVE AFTER.

Many of us struggle with waiting on God and waiting with peace. We don't trust God enough to seek understanding and wisdom to follow and abide by His will and plans for our lives. Maybe, you turned away from the will of God because it was taking too long. Because it requires patience and it doesn't move according to your timing, you may start to second-guess the will of God, and you start to entertain the idea that maybe this is not Gods plans for my life because is it not coming to fruition.

We have to learn the power of waiting. If whatever you're praying for takes months or years. Will you wait on God? I've discovered that my disobedience not only affects me and my progress, but it also affects the people around me. Especially the people who I love the most. By not waiting, I often find myself at a dead end. Now, I'm back at the beginning, torn, praying to God for direction and clarity. The same direction and clarity that He gave me already, but I chose to take the detour for the quick fixes and to think I was going to get a better outcome. Thinking I had it all figured out. Now I'm here once again back at the beginning praying for God's help, direction, forgiveness, peace, and clarity. Forgiveness for leaning towards my own understanding and not trusting Him enough to direct my path.

As I stated earlier, my disobedient has not only hurt me, but others. For example, God told me in January 2018 to stand still and to wait on Him and not date. So, I cut everyone off that I was talking to. Although I wasn't in a committed relationship, I didn't want to lead anyone on or create false hope. I didn't

Love After...

want any noise or any distractions. I wanted to solely hear from God and follow the path that He set out for me. Comes April, four months later, I started to date again not thinking it'll go anywhere. I kept telling myself there's no harm in getting to know someone. I'm just dating to keep myself occupied and not die from boredom. Well, feelings got involved, and before I knew it, things were moving faster than I anticipated. Now, this man is head over heels in love with me, talking about my ring size and engagement. I know God told me to stand still and wait on Him, but now I'm conflicted, and I'm at a crossroad. Feelings are involved, but God told me to be still and avoid relationships. So now what am I supposed to do?

Not wanting to hurt anyone's feelings, I continued to date him, not knowing I was making his feelings a priority over God's. It came to a point where, come hell or high water, I had to break it off because my peace of mind and being able to sleep at night was at stake. So, it all boiled down to me choosing my peace of mind and God's direction which is the direction I should've chosen from the beginning. Now, looking back months later, I realize my disobedience not only hurt me but also hurt him. I told him God wants me to stand still and not date because I'm still healing.

There were areas in my life still under-developed and not yet ready for a new relationship or marriage. He couldn't make sense of it initially, and he felt we could still work on ourselves while being together. I'm sure that's possible as well. However, it's bigger than the possibilities. It was about my obedience and trusting God's direction and divine timing. My wait and my obedience were more significant than him and I, and our circumstances. So, I say this to encourage you to wait on God and to be obedient. Your obedience is more significant than you, and your disobedience can cost you everything.

Many people wonder why they can't find someone to love them the right way or the way they need to be loved. Well, the first question to ask ourselves is, why do we keep attracting the same people with different names, different faces, and swag? Everyone who we've attracted has similarities that are a mirror of ourselves. We will attract who we are, what we've learned, and experienced. The only way we can attract the right person is to start changing ourselves for the better. It brings me back to the topic of healing and becoming whole.

Love After...

It's important to be complete within yourself, so you're not seeking to fill this void that you have within. When two whole and healed individuals joined together, it's not to complete but to complement each other. You'll feel free in that relationship. The relationship you have with yourself will speak volumes to a person you attract and how they will love you. Until you're right within, you will not attract the right one. Someone who is whole and healed has the wisdom and discernment to know when another is still hurting and not fully healed. So, it will be hard to attract someone who is whole until you become whole. That's why 'hurt people hurt people' because that's who you'll keep attracting.

As you heal, pray for God to open your spiritual eyes and the discernment to know when someone or something doesn't feel or seem right—then, exit right away. To love them from a distance but still pray for them. Take it as a lesson and move on. Don't allow yourself to stay and fall in deep if you feel the relationship will compromise yourself and your happiness.

When you start seeing yourself as royalty, whole, healed, complete and perfect, you will know that you are worthy and deserving. That's when you will attract the person who is in alignment with your purpose. He or she will love you the way you need to be loved. He or she will Love you like Christ loved the church. So free yourself and free your mind. In freedom, I lost everything, but gained myself! Although my back may be slouched at times, I'm still standing.

On my journey of waiting, I've discovered that our sexuality is a reminder that we were not created to be alone. Our body will naturally crave and lust after another. We may not understand the mystery around our sexuality. God did create us to be sexual beings. Sex is compelling and easily underestimated. When you have sex with someone, you are becoming one not only in the flesh but one spiritually. You're tapping into powers that are bigger than you.

Why do you think soul ties are so hard to break? Why do you think there is such a thin line between lust and love? The two are easily confused based on our energy, emotions, and our feelings. When I began to understand the power behind sex and the force behind spirits and orgasms, I had a new understanding of why God wants us to wait on marriage before we have sex. Soul ties are tough to break. Many of us have wasted countless times in unhealthy relationship due to this strong soul tie connection that was hard to break away from. We know how unhealthy this relationship is for us, but there's a strong magnetic force to this person that's hard to break. It was through the strength of God that gave me the courage to leave unhealthy relationships, despite how deep my love was. I prayed for God to break the chains of the relationship and for Him to bless me with wisdom, courage and the strength to leave and stay out.

I'm still learning, growing, and stretching as I embrace my new beginning and season. One thing I can say is, I no longer live in regret because every mistake and wrong decision that I've made have molded me and prepared me for my next step and my next season. I finally realized that all the pain was necessary for growth.

Just know that all things will work together for our good according to God's purpose for our lives. There's a purpose behind my hurt, my disappointment, the good, the bad and the ugly. When I look over my life and start to reflect, it's crazy how I realize that I'm no longer the person I was yesterday, last year, five years ago, or ten years ago. I love the new me. I love my growth, and I love my evolution.

Try this exercise:

1. Make a list of what you're looking for in a spouse and be bold and intentional about what you need. As you write, imagine that you're living with that person right now. You could even light your favorite candle and play some romantic music, to set the mood, to help you visualize.

2. In writing this list, keep in mind morals, values, spirituality, standards, boundaries, your kid(s) if any. Think about your love languages.

3. If you don't know your love languages, I'd suggest you take the 5 love languages quiz online asap (www.5lovelanguages.com) and read the *5 Love Languages* book by Gary Chapman. It will change your life and your mindset on how you need to be loved and how to love your partner effectively.

CHAPTER TWELVE

IT WAS NECESSARY

All the deaths that I've experienced were necessary for molding me into the woman I am today. Death included: divorce, molestation, suicidal thoughts, depression, anger, abuse, and all my hurts and pains. These deaths were necessary for preparing me for where I am heading. If you can't make it through minor hurdles, there's no way you can make it through the major obstacles and setbacks. To go to the next level and stand through your storms, there are some things you may have to face. Be strong, focus, and don't waiver. Be a water walker, trust God, and stand on His promises. I've learned to embrace my deaths because they molded and shaped me into the woman I am today.

I want to let you know that you're not here today by mistake. Your life and your circumstances are not a mistake. God has been with you from the beginning. Everything was predestined and planned before you were formed in your mother's womb. A lot of the detours in our lives can be avoided by walking in His will and being obedient. When you invest in yourself and your spiritual development, God will blow your mind beyond what you can imagine. The Bible says that they that hunger and thirst after righteousness shall be filled. Therefore, if you seek God, you will never grow hungry, weary, and thirsty again. My desire for Him overtakes my hunger for anything else. You'll get hit with some blows, and you will get caught with some challenges but most importantly never stop running the race or moving forward.

Continue to stand, continue to fight. Time is of the essence. God's timing is essential because it's necessary for Him to prepare your spirit for where He's taking you.

When your faith is stripped away, it changes how you view things. It changes how you react to things. You'll find that when you retrace your life, and you look back there was one incident that you've experienced that changed the dynamic of your whole life. It was like a snowball/domino effect on what is to come in your life. I once allowed my deaths to strip me from my faith and my hope. You will get to a point in your life where it's impossible for you to spring into your next season unless you clean out your past falls. Sometime God will strip certain things from your life so that you can see that all your help comes from Him. God is a jealous God, and often we put more faith and praises in our job, career, friendship, relationship, house or houses, cars, etc. Sometimes God will remove certain people from your life if you begin to worship them more than you worship Him. God wants to have you to a point where you solely rely on Him. He wants to know that you trust Him despite your circumstances. If I lose my job today, God I still trust you.

If it's your will for me to leave this relationship, God I still trust you. If I found out that I have cancer or diabetes, God I still trust you. I'll still have faith, and I'll put in the necessary work that's in my control and watch you work and perform a miracle. It doesn't matter what it looks like, what it feels like, what it sounds like, God I still trust you.

No more religion. It's time to have a relationship. So many people are so caught up in religion and going to church faithfully, but Monday to Saturday, their life is a complete wreck. Deep down they are confused, bitter, guarded and waiting for God to do a miraculous thing although they lack faith and hope. We all know faith without works is dead. You absolutely must put in the work. The work is necessary. The work goes with your purpose.

Isolation is necessary for elevation. We all pray for this Abrahamic blessing. Keep in mind, for Abraham to receive that mega blessing God had in store for him, he needed to leave and be isolated. Leave behind and separate yourself from all the negativity and leave behind what makes you comfortable and complacent.

At one point I felt so alone. Although I wasn't alone and I had people around me, I still felt lonely, and I didn't feel like anyone around me fully understood me. That's the lie the enemy fed me. Then as I grew in my relationship with God, I became more spiritually mature. Now I can understand that God kept me hidden because he didn't want everyone to see me while under development. There are some things that God must work through behind closed doors to mold and shape you in private before he can display it in public. You don't want to do anything prematurely. That's why it's important to trust the process and trust divine timing. Everything isn't meant to put on social media. Not everything you need to tell your friends, family, or companions. God has you hidden for a reason. *Trust Him.* I had to find peace in standing still. There were seasons that I had to endure where I felt like my life was at a complete standstill. I wasn't doing bad, yet I wasn't doing good, because I wasn't where I needed to be in my life as I got older. Have you ever been lost and confused in that gray area of your life, the in-between? What do you do when you feel stuck? It's a very confusing position to be in.

I just felt stuck and didn't know what to do next. Then one day I began to fast, pray, and cry in frustration to God. That's when the Lord told me; *I need you to be at peace with standing still.* Don't worry about your delays because I'm going to expedite you to where I can get the glory. However, before that, there are still some areas I need to develop and mold before I transition you into my next season. Then my lightbulb went off, and I had my 'Aha' moment. I realized I just wasn't ready, and I would not be effective in my purpose had I shifted prematurely. I don't want to be a preemie. That's when I learned that the process is necessary. It may not feel good to me, but it's good for me. God is trying to build us, stretch us, and mold us. God wants to know that He can trust us with the assignment.

While you're waiting, standing still, and being hidden allow God to shift your perspective, shift your heart, shift your mindset, and shift your faith. When you get out of your way and stop comparing yourself, stop seeking validation, and accept what God has in stores for you, then you can arrive and be in alignment for the blessings God has in store for you. God wants to separate you so that He can elevate you. There's power in being hidden. There's power in your silence. There's power in being still.

Some of you may feel like God has forgotten about you. He hasn't. Your vision is just blurry with anger, setbacks, betrayal, hurt, bad habits, and bad company. Most times, you're in your own way. I pray that all our pains and anger will be removed and replaced with worship, joy, thanksgiving, and an active prayer life. I pray that you will begin to see clearly from a new perspective. God, I pray that you clear our lens from all distractions and place our focus on you. I pray that we will stand on your promises and strengthen our faith in your word that whatever you promise us and planted inside of us will be birth into existence.

Learn to have Thanksgiving in your spirit. If He does nothing else give Him thanks and love Him just because He's a sovereign God. Even when you are going

Love After...

through your valleys of darkness, do not fear and trust Him. Do not fear but rise with power and authority to take back what the enemy stole from you and receive everything God has in stores for you.

CHAPTER THIRTEEN

BIRTHING YOUR PURPOSE

God is a God that will speak to the dry and dead places in your life. He's resurrecting those dry places, your vision, your finances, your dreams, your relationships, your family, and your career. He will resurrect certain areas in your life that have been lying dormant for a while. God wants us to live a more abundant life. Well, happy birthday. It's time to come alive and birth those visions out of you. I know you're hurting, you're in pain and been crying countless nights.

Dry your eyes, because weeping may endure for a night but joy cometh in the morning (Psalms 30:5). God wants you to deliver these babies He has planted inside of you. So, get out of the operating room and go into the recovery room. It's time to start living. Those things that you thought were dead are not dead. They've just been asleep. You might think your babies a.k.a. your visions and dreams are dead but— newsflash-- they're not dead. It's Resurrection time. It's time to invite the Lord into those vulnerable areas in your life, into your heart, and allow him to resurrect those areas to make you whole. God has the final say and is turning those things around right now.

There is LOVE AFTER YOUR DEATHS!

Do you ever wonder why at first when you're pregnant, you can't physically see that you're pregnant, but you know you're pregnant according to what the doctor says or according to the test results? Think of that in the spiritual realm. God is trying to impregnate us with visions, dreams, and purpose. However, because we can't see the manifestation and the work that He's doing in the physical, we tend to get frustrated. So, by being impatient, we put ourselves at risk to miss the seed that God's trying to plant in us.

You have to operate with a 'right now' spirit and praise Him in advance for what He's doing and about to do in your life. You may not be able to see it, but that doesn't mean he's not shifting, molding and transitioning somethings in your life. Often God is just waiting for you to get out of your way and say 'yes' to His will and 'no' to setbacks you're entertaining in the space He's trying to bless. It's easy to block your blessings if you are not careful.

Although you can't see it, you need to learn to trust the process. It's time to prep, transition, and shift yourself to give birth to your purpose that He has planted inside of you. It's manifestation season!

Love After...

CHAPTER FOURTEEN

FIRST TRIMESTER OF PURPOSE

The first trimester is the most critical because this is when you get impregnated with your vision or seed. This is when all the major organs and the nervous system are formed. This is *the* trimester where most miscarriages and abortions happen. You must be extra careful with the seed inside you. This is when you're most delicate and vulnerable. This is where a lot of people are ready to give up and throw in the towel. In your first trimester, you'll also have memories and thoughts rising to the surface that you've never dealt with. God will move certain things out of your way, so your deaths can rise to the surface, so you are forced to deal with them.

Certain things will rise to the surface that you didn't even think you were struggling with. You've allowed these things to lay dormant. You made the decision not to deal with them. Now years, months, and weeks have passed, and you've just become so immune to the pain that you forgot why you are hurting. You'll find yourself in this trimester masking or covering up your pain with a smile.

You may have tried to hide your problems by being cordial and think if you keep a smile on your face, you'll look like you have it all together. Sometimes, you got to have those ugly cries so you can release and begin evolving. One time, I was standing in aisle five at Walmart with tears flowing down my face. I had to let it happen because if I kept it bottled up, I knew I would lash out on the ones closest to me.

Accept and understand that we are human and we're not perfect. So, it's okay to cry and let it out so you can let it go. You never know who might see you crying, and that same person will share words of encouragement tied to your purpose. We have to get out of this mindset in which, we are so guarded that we can't afford to let anybody see us sweat or breakdown. There are many people who love you and will intercede on your behalf.

We're human, and it's okay to be vulnerable. Put your pride to the side. Just be true to yourself as you live moment by moment. I'm here to tell you in the middle of your breakdown-- trust God. It's just amazing how it all work together for our good. How all

Love After...

these moving pieces from our past, present, and future all ties together to make this one finished piece called purpose. You might be asking or thinking life isn't worth living, but the fact that you're still here is a testament letting you know that you have yet to complete your purpose and God isn't through with you. Just trust the process; trust Him and His timing.

Don't be distracted by your current circumstances. It doesn't matter what it feels like or looks like, because the plans that God has for your life will come to pass. God can still use your mess for *His* glory. I say that because most people think they must be perfect and flawless to be used by God. Your flaws and your imperfection are a part of your purpose. Your life and your breakthrough are an example for others who can relate to you and will be used as a blessing to them.

Part of your purpose is being relatable to the people you're purposed to help. Go back to the beginning, to the promises that God shared with you. Go back to the seed and the vision that God planted inside of you. Trust the birthing process. Stop aborting your blessings. It's time to push forward. It's time for your seed to grow. It's time to start watering the seed and standing on the promises that God gave you.

CHAPTER FIFTEEN

SECOND TRIMESTER OF PURPOSE

The second trimester is where you accept yourself, flaws and all. You come out of hiding. You are ready to take the mask off and peel the Band-Aid off your womb. You need to be prepared to be naked--withholding nothing in order for God to strip you of all these deaths that have kept you dormant and stagnant. You are ready, and standing firm no longer wavering but prepared to be used by God.

In this trimester you will begin to see things shift as you start renewing your mindset. According to Romans 12:2(ESV) God said, *"Do not be conformed to this world, but be transformed by the renewing of your mind. Then you will be able to discern what is the good, pleasing, and perfect will of God."*

When I was pregnant, it was in my second trimester I started noticing the growth of my baby bump. People began to notice that I was pregnant. People began to see the changes in my body, and they started to notice my pregnancy glow. The second trimester is more comfortable because you're no longer battling with the morning sickness of lies, self-doubt, deceit, unforgiveness, and you know who you are and you know your worth. You are starting to transform into the newer you. You are more at peace, and you're starting to figure everything out and why the process was so necessary.

The journey of healing, becoming whole, and finding your purpose all starts from the renewing of your mind. The mind is so powerful. When you think about it, the enemy attacks us first through our mind. For example, suicide and addictions all start from our thoughts before we act on them. In this season I had to fight hard to get my mind right. I had to fight hard to get my heart right, and I constantly prayed for God to not only renew my mind but to create in me a clean heart.

To give me a new perspective on how to view life and a new perspective on what love truly is. I know going into my new season, I had to find a new meaning of love because the meaning I had was now destroyed and tampered with. I was naked and ready to be used by God, flaws and all. Although I didn't trust, I was ready to learn how to be used by God. In this trimester

I was ready to fight hard like a roaring lion and ready to take back everything the enemy stole from me. Ready to fight like my life depended on it because it did. I was finally ready to live and no longer exist. This trimester is where I had to learn to start forgiving my offenders. I had to trust God that all of this was going to work out for my good. So far, the good that came out of it was my *Love After* purpose and birthing out this Love After book. My advice to anyone reading this book is, know and believe there is Love After your deaths.

Trust God and the process. Get up and dust yourself off. God's not done with you yet. Put your hand over your heart, and you'll feel that your heart is still beating. You're still breathing. That means that you're still alive and if God was done with you, you wouldn't still be here today. You could've gotten into a car accident on your way home. You could've died from unknown causes. You could've died from a sickness you're struggling with. You could have been killed by a stray bullet or poisoned. Not to scare you but just want to remind you that you never know which day is your last day.

At one point in my life, I was taking life for granted and didn't care whether I was alive or not.

Love After...

There were times when I didn't feel the need to live. That's how dead I was on the inside. I started having suicidal thoughts and didn't feel like life was worth living anymore. I didn't want to get out of the bed. I didn't feel like eating like I usually would. I hated when the light shined through my windows. My room always had to be dark. Now looking back, I'm now thinking how selfish of me that was. My life doesn't belong to me, and my purpose is not about me. My mission is more significant than me. Thank God for keeping me even when I didn't deserve to be kept.

I thank Him daily for His grace and His undeserving mercies. Anything that was keeping me from building a relationship with God and preventing me from walking in my purpose had to go. I was super sensitive and allergic to anything that cost me my peace of mind.

Now, as you begin to walk in your new season and experiencing your love after journey, people will try you. Don't allow anyone to kill your spirit or your joy. I pray against those spiritual attacks in the name of Jesus. Don't allow anyone to put you back in the grave. We come against temptations and the need to feel like you have to defend yourself.

Some people will think you've changed and are acting brand new.

Yes, I had to make changes to shift my mindset and my priorities. You can either love me or learn to love me where I am. If not pray for me. Don't allow anyone to assassinate what God is trying to birth out of you. Some people will try to pull you back to where you've died from. Don't let anyone or anything put you back in that grave. The Lord is your defender. You don't have to defend yourself against no one. If people love you and respect you, they'll accept or pray for you out of love. If you don't give someone the power to upset, bother, or intimidate you, then they'll have no control over your life.

I've learned you have to teach people how to treat you because people will do to you what you allow them to. That comes with setting boundaries because you have full control, power, and authority over your space and the energy you allow around you. You can't entirely blame some of your offenders if they showed you who they were, but you still entertained them. They showed you their true colors, but you chose to be colorblind. We have to learn to take responsibility for our actions and take our power back. I choose to not allow anyone

Love After...

to disrespect me. You may not like me or agree with me, and that's okay. I will embrace our differences with respect.

CHAPTER SIXTEEN

THIRD TRIMESTER OF PURPOSE

In this trimester, you are more confident of who you are and whose you are. You've made it through the first two trimesters, and you didn't abort or miscarry. You were able to weather the storms, and you are still standing. In this trimester you know what your purpose is, and you understand why you had to go through your trials and tribulation. You now understand why it was all necessary and that everything will work out for your good.

My third trimester was when I noticed my growth. I was stronger spiritually, mentally, emotionally, and most of all forgiving. I found myself trying to make peace and genuinely forgive anyone that offended me, both directly and indirectly. I knew I had truly forgiven people when I was able to pray for them even after they hurt me. I truly wanted to see them prosper. To not only forgive but to pray for them, shows a lot of growth and maturity. God wants to birth greatness out of you. Birthing requires you to push through the pain, push through the contractions, push through the hurt, push through the headaches, the heartaches, the pain, push through feelings of inadequacy and defeat, push through loneliness, push through financial difficulties, push through the naysayers, liars, push through deceit, push through addictions, push through molestation and rape and push through your deaths. I know you're tired. I understand your contractions hurt, but you have to *PUSH*.

Don't fight against others while God is fighting your battles. Ephesians 6:10-13 ESV states, *Finally, be strong in the Lord and in the strength of His might. Put on the whole armor of God, that you may be able to stand against the schemes of the devil. <u>For we do not wrestle against flesh and blood</u>, but against the rulers, against the authorities, against the cosmic powers over this present darkness, against the spiritual forces of evil in the heavenly places. Therefore, take up the whole armor of God, that you may <u>be able to withstand in the evil day</u>, and having done all, to <u>stand firm.</u>*

We are aware that we don't fight or wrestle against flesh and blood. We must wrestle and push against the tactics of the enemy. It's a spiritual battle.

It's time to conceive the treasure that God planted in you. When you finally give birth to this treasure, the vision, your purpose, everything in you and around will change to conform to your new season and identity. You will begin to see things manifest that you never thought would come true or come to pass. I pray that you will birth out gifts, visions, talents, businesses, creative ideas, ministry, and stand with authority and power. Do you know how powerful you are and how much Authority God has given you? It's time that we walk with authority and power. Push! Push! Push!

I had to stand boldly without fear or compromise to push out my new beginning. My new beginning was based on following my dreams, my new journey with Christ and finally saying yes to myself. Loving me more and choosing myself doesn't mean that I love the people around me any less. Many people couldn't accept the new me because they couldn't understand my growth and where God was taking me. God was transforming me in private with no interference. One of the best decisions I've ever made was learning to say 'yes' to myself and to love myself more.

Some people in your life will not be able to accept the new you. Maybe, they're not equipped and or in

Love After...

alignment with God's will or His purpose for your life. This was a rude awakening because the more I grow and the higher I climb; the more people were becoming more distant. Everything in me wanted everyone in my life to support me on my new journey through life-- but they couldn't. I had to learn that they couldn't go with me because my relationship with them reflected who I was and where I was in my past life. We are what we attract --- the law of attraction.

This trimester is when I learned about the different seasons in my life. I also began to understand why certain people are only meant to be in your life for a season or reason. I had to learn to embrace the end of the season to fully accept the beginning of the new season in my life. This is how I knew whether I was out of alignment. Just like the changes in the seasons, spring, summer, fall, winter, we are going to have to change accordingly to the weather forecast in our lives.

In each season you will have to shed dead weight and clean house as a preparation. Just like when a woman is pregnant, she goes through this nesting phase. She starts to prepare for her baby. It's time to clean house and prepare for your blessings and your new season. Any relationship that cannot grow with you will either evolve or dissolve.

It's time to shift your mindset, your perspective, and your faith. It's time to shift from how you used to think and feel towards life. Your beliefs and your faith carry the power that God placed on the inside of you. When everything around you is saying 'no,' the same belief and faith will put a 'yes' in your spirit. Even when it doesn't look right, feel right, or seems right, you're still standing on God's promises with a yes in your spirit. I trust and believe you'll never leave me or forsake me. Yes, I believe that I am more than a conqueror. I believe that I am the head, not the tail, above and not beneath, a leader, not a follower, a lender not a borrower. Even though you can't see it as yet, hold on to His promises. I promise you the wait is worth it. You can't be afraid and have faith at the same time. You can't have forgiveness and bitterness at the same time. It's like oil and water they won't mix. We walk by faith and not by sight.

If you are reading this book, you may be feeling burdened down, empty, broken, frustrated, desperate for a change, tired, hurt and angry. You may feel like life isn't worth living and asking why am I here? God wants you to know that everything that you need,

Love After...

desire and are seeking is within Him. Allow Him to be your refuge and your Safe Haven.

Seek Him first, and all things will be added unto you. Get to know Him for yourself intimately and tap into His presence daily. There's nothing God will not do for you. He is omnipresent, omnipotent, and omniscient. Don't allow the enemy to steal your joy and confuse the promises that God has given you. He's waiting on you to push and give birth to His promises and to give birth to everything He told you he'd do for you. It's time to give birth to your purpose.

"Happy Birthday!"
We're free!
We know who we are and whose we are.
We feel complete, and we know we are ENOUGH.
We've embraced our uniqueness, flaws and all.
The good, the bad, and the ugly.

CHAPTER SEVENTEEN

TAKING OUR POWER BACK

Have you ever been so busy to the point where you're exhausted, but nothing is getting accomplished?

Do you feel like a hamster on a wheel, running but heading nowhere? Although I wear many hats, I am so grateful for all my blessings. I am just at a point in my life where I don't want to settle for safe and live life in the gray area anymore. I want everything that God promised me, but I must first get in alignment. I keep busy doing my motherly duties and making sure my kids get to and from school, to and from Girl Scouts, and to football practice and games. Making sure I continue to do a fantastic job as a QVC model, which is a huge blessing for me, my kids and my finances.

I'm continually auditioning, either doing a self-tape or driving to New York City to audition in person. When I book a role, then I'm on set working. Then at one point, I was trying to date, and trying to keep up with that became somewhat exhausting. Then trying to have social time with my friends and trying to network

Love After...

for my business. Then I go to church on Sundays to release all my burdens and worship with thanksgiving.

I list my daily routine because I wanted to show you that I had all of this going on but still felt like something was missing. Don't get me wrong; I am in a much better place in my life than I've ever been before but something still felt off. I felt powerless. I felt like I was still running on the wheel. It was in September 2018, I just broke down one day and lost it. In the blink of an eye after all this work I've done I was ready to give up on everything because I was drained and felt like I wasn't getting anywhere. So, I did what I knew best, which was to get in the presence of God to seek clarity and direction. I started fasting, praying and staying in His presence until I got an answer. Then the Lord answered and told me I was blocking my blessings. He said, *"daughter I gave you the vision but out of fear you keep detouring. I need you to give me full access if you trust me. You want me to navigate and drive, but you still have your foot on the brakes. If you want me to navigate and control the vehicle you have to sit in the passenger seat."* As easy as this sounds, it was the hardest thing for me to do.

From that day forward, I made a vow with God

that I'm going to trust Him and allow Him to navigate my life fully. I am going to have faith and not fear. I am not going to worship yet still worry. It's like oil and water-- they don't mix. We have to choose a side and stick to it. You can't have one foot in and one foot out. It's all or nothing. You either stay seated in fear and worry or take a leap of faith and jump with trust. I refused to be a hamster on a wheel, and I was ready to take my power back. I was ready to step out on faith and follow the vision God gave me without looking back. I was no longer going to do anything outside of the instructions He gave me. He told me to wait on Him and date Him.

I took dating off the table in obedience. He told me to finish my *Love After* book and put it out in February, the month of love, and that's what I'm doing. He told me to create my own content and produce my films, and that's what I'm doing. I got tired of having my success riding on someone else's yes. I got tired of waiting for the words, "you booked it!" from my agents, in order to feel accomplished. I am ready to take my power back and walk boldly in my purpose.

When I decided to shift to the passenger seat and take my hands off the steering wheel, my foot off the

Love After...

brake and gas pedal was when I started to see God do miraculous things in my life. I knew this Love After vision was bigger than me, but I didn't know how it was going to get done with limited funds and resources. I wish I could sit here and write that I have all the answers and I have it all figured out, but I'd be lying. However, the only thing I need to know is that I am trusting God. Fear and worries have taken a backseat, and I am solely walking out on faith like a water walker. That's the recipe to living your life in peace while walking in your purpose.

When you trust and believe in God, whatever it is that your heart desires and if it aligns according to God's will, He will send the right people on your journey to help you. God will provide the resources and the support system that you need for your assignment and your purpose. He will send people that you've never met before who will come in your life to assist in the manifestation of the vision and to accomplish the assignment. I thank God for the lovely Jane Applegate, my manager, who I met on the set of a TV pilot she produced a few years ago. She came on board selflessly, and has been willing to do anything necessary to help me birth this vision into the world.

She edited this book and is producing a short film about my life (directed by her talented friend, JP Pacca). She's also helping me produce my international book tour and the sequel to my first feature film. Jane provides support for me every day. She's a complete blessing, and I can't find enough words or actions to thank her enough.

I also thank God for Andrée Harris, who I've met on a TV pilot I was producing, and for her team at Infinity Publications, LLC. They've played a huge role in making this book a reality, along with Antoine Allen, who've motivated me to write this book and to tell my story through both literature and film.

As a first-time author, they held my hand and patiently guided me through the process. It's not easy to write a book and let everyone into your life, but they encouraged me and kept me calm with limited anxiety.

I am at peace with waiting, being still, and being hidden until God finds it fit to bring me out and give me His platform. If one person reads this book and become free, healed, whole, and can now walk in his or her purpose, I'm at peace. We often block our blessings because we fear the unknown and whether others will support us. I had to get to a place of peace and

Love After...

contentment. I can't worry about the numbers and how successful it's going to be or not going to be. All I can worry about is what's in my control and the things I can change. Which is being obedient and following the vision that God gave me.

Now I can see my relationship with God is the strongest that it has ever been. I am walking in my purpose even though this is just the beginning. I've released this book, and I no longer have control of what happens, but I have faith that it's going to do what it's intended to do. I am praying about my vision of producing a film based on or inspired by this book. I am planning to have an annual empowerment conference, where people can be healed, delivered, set free, find their purpose, find their inner strength to jump and take their power back.

It'll be a two-day experience like never before in which you'll die to self and die from whatever deaths that are holding you captive with shackles of feeling ashamed, inadequate, insecure, lost, and feeling like you're not enough. Then, on the second day, we are going to find our love after, find true selves and our new beginnings. We're going to leave this conference knowing what our purpose is and how to fulfill our vision. I'm ready for all of us to take our power back!

CHAPTER EIGHTEEN

THE POWER OF PRAYER

Prayer is the way we communicate with God. There is Power in Prayer. Prayer changes things. Prayer is not optional-- it's necessary. Prayer is the air that you breathe. It's how you build intimacy with God. It's communion and communication with God. That's where you connect and hear from God. Some may think prayer has to look a certain way, sound a certain way, be a certain length, or even feel a certain way, but prayer merely is just communication with our Heavenly Father.

How do you communicate with God?
You can talk to God anytime and anywhere, and God will always hear you. Just talk, cry, whisper, yell, laugh, etc. I pray in my bed, in the shower, in my car, on my couch, while I'm cooking and cleaning. I talk to Him like I would talk to my best friend because He is. I'm so grateful for my grandmother's prayers. I'm still riding on her prayers and reaping her blessings. I haven't come across any prayer warrior like my Grand-

Love After...

ma Lucilda, who is 93 years old. I am so grateful and privileged to have her in my life, along with other friends and families who intercedes on my behalf.

There were times when I felt like my prayers were falling on deaf ears, and God wasn't hearing me. Looking back, now I know where I went wrong. I was praying, but I stopped believing. I was praying, but I didn't have patience. I moved according to my own understandings.

Philippians 4:6-7 (ESV) states, *"Do not be anxious about anything, but in everything by prayer and supplication with thanksgiving, let your request be made known to God; and the peace of God, which surpasses all understanding, will guard your hearts and minds through Christ Jesus."* No matter how broken you are right now, God can and will do something extraordinary with your life.

When we lack prayer and communication with God, we find ourselves in relationships we shouldn't be in, addicted to things that shouldn't have control over us, and being led by our fleshly desires. These then become the things that drive us and not our desires of God. The problem is the things we seek will never fill that void that only God can fill. You'll try, but then you'll get to a point in your life where you are exhausted and ready to throw in the towel, and that's when we are reminded that it wasn't God's will in the first place. We've been living according to our will while seeking our desires.

There are times when I get swamped and overwhelmed that I don't spend enough quality time in the presence of God. I'll pray a quick prayer when I get up or in my car driving to work or while I'm in the shower just to say, *'thank you.'* Although some communication is better than none, God still wants to know that He is a priority. If we can take time out to binge watch our favorite shows, stay up sleepless nights for our career, spend hours on the phone, and hours hanging out with our friends, then we can spend the same amount of time hanging out with God. He's a jealous God, and He craves our attention as well. I know when I haven't been in His presence like I'm supposed to because I can feel the difference. I'd feel more stressed, more burden down, more emotional, more on edge, and I lack peace. If you're too busy wearing multiple hats, that's all the reason you should seek God in prayer and fasting. So that God can navigate everything in your life effortlessly and you won't go crazy with being overwhelmed and have anxiety attacks. I want to have peace and joy. Peace comes with spending quality time with God and constantly checking in.

We have to pray more and complain less. I had to learn to spend less time on my phone complaining and talking about things that aren't productive and spend more time praying. I don't know if you've seen the movie *"War Room"* by Alex Kendrick. Ever since I saw that movie, I quickly created a praying area where I can spend intimate time with God and meditate in him.

If you haven't, please watch this movie. It will change your life and your perspective. If you've ever questioned the power of prayer, this movie will change your whole perception. When you begin to pray and declare things in your life, you will begin to see things shift.

We all have direct access to God, for grace, mercy, favor, blessings, and direction. Some people feel like they need to go to a psychic or fortune teller for tarot card or palm readings to learn about the life God gave us. Seek your creator. I've learned these psychics can never be as accurate as God. When I was lost and didn't know how to hear directly from God, I thought that God would hear my prayers more if it's coming from a bishop, pastor, or minister. I even went to see a Tarot card reader, in the hope of getting clarity and direction from her. By the end of the reading, she only confirmed what I already knew, and some of the things she told me didn't happen the way she predicted or never happened at all.

God flagged me for that. I started to feel convicted for seeking and trusting someone else over Him. There were times in my life when I didn't know or understand how to pray effectively and didn't have the strength to pray. In that case, God has servants who will step in and intercede on your behalf and stand in the gap for you. When you get through, you'll appreciate those prayers and intercessors.

When I began to turn my life around and was going through my Love After Death transformation, I had to change my mindset and stop giving people more access and power over God. Be careful who you allow to speak over your life. Life and death lie in the power of the tongue. Allow God to be your fortune teller. The Bible clearly tells us in Deuteronomy 18:10-11(ESV), that we are to avoid anyone *"who practices divination or sorcery, tell fortunes, interprets omens, engages in witchcraft, cast spells, or who is a medium or spiritist who consults the dead."* They contradict the honor, respect, faith, and loving fear that we owe to God and Him alone. You have direct access to God. Also, you don't need to solely rely on a priest for your prayers to be heard. No one holds more power that our God Almighty. Seek your creator directly for the wisdom and direction you need for your life. God will guide you as you make decisions about your future. He loves us and wants to see us prosper and make Him proud.

Just because someone is saved and decided to give their life to Christ, that doesn't mean that they're exempt from having issues and struggles in their lives. I stay prayed up continually, so I don't react out of frustration. Being saved and single can be very challenging. So, prayer helps me to control myself and my mind. Prayer helps me to not operate out of my fleshly and lustful desires, anger and frustration. I constantly seek communication with God as He continuously works in me. We are all a work in progress, saved or unsaved.

Once we hear God speak, it's time to move. The

problem is we don't always obey or like to change. There are some things that God wants to do to free us from our burdens and concerns, but we must trust God and move according to His will for your life. Sometimes it's hard to pray and hear God's voice louder than your circumstances. We've all been there, and I know it's hard. We need to continue to pray until something happens, or the shifts take place. We must be very intentional to listen to the voice of God.

Listen up so we can know what He desires for us to do—to really know His plans for our lives. He will reveal it in many ways. He may reveal it in others He knows we can trust. He will reveal it in your spirit once you can hear His voice and be more in tune with Him. He will open doors when you least expect it. Just know God can make all things possible.

Let the Holy Spirit inside of you guide you. You will start looking and being new. You will begin to see that you no longer look like what you've been through. Whatever you want God to manifest in your life will always need to start with a prayer. Communicate your heart desires to God. Be prepared for what you've prayed for. Faith without work is dead. Pray, prepare and seek God's will in everything that you do. Then put

Love After...

in the work and be ready for your life to become better. Sharpen your tools. The more you pray, the more you will see things manifest in your life. Most importantly in addition to praying, we also will need to have faith and believe in divine timing. God is an on-time God.

I remember at one point in my life I was so obsessed with social media, that as soon as I woke up, the first thing I did was check Instagram and Facebook notifications before I checked in with God. I was more concerned about my connection with people in my network than my connection with my creator. Then I just got sick and tired of social media, and I had to pray and fast against it. Social media is so powerful and easily underestimated. I would get on Instagram and by the time I blink two hours passed, and I had nothing to show for it, or nothing accomplished. I was quickly losing time that I couldn't get back.

I prayed for God to take this distraction away and then took a two-month fast from social media.
I deactivated my accounts and took the apps off my phone. After my two-month fast, I have since limited myself on social media. Unfortunately, to market and promote yourself as an artist, there's no getting around social media. Before you get hired or book for some

jobs, people first want to see your social media handle. People are more invested in your social media than getting to know you the actual person and your capabilities. I still believe any blessings that God has in stores for you will come to fruition with or without social media. God has the final say, Period!

    Pray more until it becomes a bad habit and a lifestyle change. You will get to a place in your life where you cannot do anything without first communicating with God.

Where is your communication and connection with God?

_____

_____

_____

    If you haven't already, try to find a room, a private area, or even a corner that you can use as your daily prayer and meditation area. You can put down blankets, pillows, your favorite candles, your holy oil, whatever's going to create the atmosphere and set the energy for prayer, meditation, and worship.

    You can get some sticky notes and pen or sharpie and write positive re-affirmations daily and stick them in this area or anywhere as you're led. On those sticky notes, you can also write down people or things that you want to pray for and that you want God's help to fix or change.

As you begin to witness God answering your prayers, I want you to start putting checkmarks. Over a period, you will begin to see how many prayers and promises that God has fulfilled. It's mind-blowing to recognize and to reflect because often we forget that God does answer our prayers and fulfills His promises.

Whenever you're feeling down, and the enemy starts to fill your mind with doubts and the lack of faith and hope, you need to look at your sticky notes with the checkmarks and constantly remind yourself that God is able to do exceedingly and abundantly above all you can ask, think, or even imagine. You'll notice that the job that you prayed for two months ago was fulfilled. God did that. He is our provider.

You'll see that your child that you prayed for is now healed from sickness. God is a healer. You'll notice that house that you prayed for you got it. You'll notice that spouse that you prayed for was fulfilled. You'll notice when you were struggling in your marriage, and you pray to God, He fixed it. God is our counselor.

When you couldn't get out of that bad relationship because of the soul tie and blinding love, you are now free from it. He is a deliverer. You'll notice that car accident that nearly took your life; you are now healed and fully recovered.

You'll notice that bullet that nearly took your life or your loved one's life missed, and you're still alive. Remember when the doctor told you that you were terminally ill and only had days, weeks, or only a few months left to live, but years later you're still alive? God is able and He has the final say. This will help to reprogram your mind and be a continual reminder of how awesome God is. I've searched all over, and there's nothing or no one like Him or even greater than Him.

Sometimes we get so complacent, comfortable, and exhausted, to the point we forget where God has led us. We forget that if God was able to do it before, then He can do it again. He's the same powerful and mighty God. If you trust Him and follow Him, you'll be the best you've ever been in your life going forward. When you pray to God in private, God will empower you, and bless you openly.

Spend some one on one time with God so that He can speak to your heart. God is rebuilding your hope and strength. Once you're in alignment with His will,

Love After...

you will embark upon a new season in your lives that you've never experienced before. God wants to birth something new in us. Praise God in advance for your new purpose, drive, vision, passion, and new life.

Go in with humility and go out with power!

JACINTH HEADLAM

MY PRAYER

Father God in the name of Jesus, Holy Spirit, my creator, my daddy, it's me your daughter standing in the gap interceding on behalf of everyone who has read this book, reading the book, or about to read this book. Lord God, you know what troubles their hearts. You know what plagues their mind and you know their trials and struggles. Lord, I asked that you bless them beyond what they can ask for, think of, or even imagine.

Father God, I pray right now for a miraculous breakthrough. I pray that you awaken whatever have died or lying dormant in us. Father God, I pray For Restoration and Resurrection in the name of Jesus. Lord restore everything that we've lost. Holy Spirit move as you see fit. We give you full access and permission to navigate our lives like never before. Lord your word says in Matthew 5:6, *"Blessed are those who hunger and thirst for righteousness, for they will be filled."*

So, Lord, I pray that you empty us so that you may fill us up father God. Lord, we hunger after you.

Love After...

We want more of you. I pray that you strengthen us and keep us. Lord God, I thank you for your undeserving grace and your mercy.

Lord, I declare, and I decree victory over their minds, victory over their trials, and circumstances. Victory over generational curses. Victory over doubts and feelings of inadequacy. Victory over past hurt, traumas, lies, deceit, and betrayals. We are more than a conqueror. We are victorious. We are leaders and not followers. Father God, I pray that you block any hindrance. I bind up any blessing Blockers.

Lord God, we are standing boldly and firmly on your promises for our LOVE AFTER. We pray for new love, new marriages, new levels, new seasons, new dimensions, new beginnings, new births, new blessings, newness in all the areas of our lives. We ask these things in your wonderful and precious name. We declare it so in Jesus name. Amen!

JACINTH HEADLAM

ABOUT THE AUTHOR

Jacinth Headlam is a multi-award-winning actress, model, film producer, and mother who was born and raised in St. Mary, Jamaica. She later relocated to Brooklyn, NY with the hope of creating a better life.

At 10, she dreamed of becoming a professional actress and model. Passionate, determined, and driven, Jacinth began her journey as an artist by modeling at age 17. She is now a proud QVC fashion and beauty model. She recently became a beauty model for IT Cosmetics/L'Oréal.

While in college, she discovered her love for theater. Jacinth has appeared in numerous films, commercials, web series and TV shows. She's currently appearing in Bubbly Brown Sugar, a web series currently in post- production.

In recent months, Jacinth has booked a leading role in a television pilot: "Caribbean Girls NYC." The show aired in France, Canada and throughout the Caribbean Islands on the FLOW network.

Love After...

She recently won an award for Best Leading Actress at the Philadelphia Independent Film awards 2017. She also received the People's Choice Award at the 2016 Nafca African Oscar, for her leading role in "Muda."

She also won Best Leading Actress for her leading role in "Diary of a Badman," written/directed by Diemiruaye Deniran, at the Caribbean Tales Film Festival in Toronto, Canada. "Diary of a Badman" is the first film she produced. She recently booked a principal role on an Emmy® Award winning television show, "A Crime to Remember", directed by Christopher Dillion.

Recently, she co-produced her first television pilot, "Illusions," in which she has also played a leading role.

Jacinth is a true definition of not relying on anyone for an opportunity. By producing her own films, she is not only creating opportunities for herself but most importantly for others to live out their dreams.

When she's not working on set, modeling or spending time with her two children, she loves to write screenplays and mentor adolescents with the goal of helping them fulfill their dreams and purpose.

Jacinth's goal is to be a successful, inspiring and influential award-winning actress who represents her Jamaican origins on a variety of mainstream platforms.

Please visit her website: www.iamjacinth.com
For booking information, please contact:
Jane Applegate, janewapplegate@me.com

JACINTH HEADLAM

NOTE FROM THE AUTHOR

All the good, the bad, and the ugly that you've faced in your life, I promise you, they'll work out for your good. Just continue to trust God, lean on Him and stand on His promises. He said it Himself in Jeremiah 29:11 (NCV), *"that the plan He has for your life is not to harm you but to give you hope and a future."*

Stand firm in your faith and hope. Watch God turn your trials into your testimonies and make your enemies your footstool. He will prepare your table in the presence of your enemies. Don't worry about your offenders. Just put them in God's hands. Don't worry about tomorrow. Trust God and put everything in His hands.

Please let me know if this book has helped you find a new path. I welcome all your thoughts. You can email me at: TheLoveAfter@gmail.com
Love you all & God bless,

jacinth

CREDITS

My heartfelt gratitude & appreciation to:

Jayden and Jenesis (My children)
Lucilda Jackson (Maternal Grandma)
Cecile Jackson (Mom)
Bentley Headlam (Dad)
My Families and Friends
Jane Applegate
JP Pacca
Infinity Publications, LLC.
A&R Royal Décor
Fierce Divas Pray
Kiyaana Cox-Jones
Diana Wright (R.I.P) (LWC)
Ruth Deniran
Greater Shiloh Church PA
ShootWorks Photography
JuzMania-Vikki Deniran
Stuart Cinema & Café
Johnnel Smith
Bill Medei
Belinda Washington
Aleksandr Beaudoin
David King
Courtney Patterson
Blue Photography NYC

JACINTH HEADLAM

Love After...

Made in the USA
Columbia, SC
11 March 2020